"The author does an excellent job in providing useful information to both franchisers and potential franchisees in an easy to read format. This book is a must read for anyone looking at purchasing a franchise."

Rob Lancit, Franchise Development Executive
(Founder of CANAM Franchise Development
Group)

"The author describes the important components of acquiring and operating a franchise with such detail that The Franchise Handbook *is an ideal tool for prospective franchisees."*

Ed Teixeira, President of FranchiseKnowHow
and author of *Franchising - From The Inside Out*

"Interesting and informative reading. This book has a wealth of knowledge and guidance taking it a step above what's currently available in franchise literature."

Kevin B. Murphy, B.S., M.B.A., J.D.
Mr. Franchise
Franchise Foundations

"By providing a comprehensive and daunting guide to the ins and outs of becoming a franchisee or a franchiser, this outstanding book may help both parties have a clearer understanding of the business relationship they are entering into. Franchisers could do well to oblige prospective franchisees to read this book before making a potentially painful mistake."

Robert Bartlett, Partner, BJA
Retail Management Consultants

"This book provides prospective franchisees and franchisers alike with an exceptionally detailed road map for buying or starting a franchise system. This well-written and well-documented book should be required reading for anyone considering the biggest investment of his or her life."

Rob Bond, President of Source Book
Publications and author of over 10 books on
franchising

"I found your book to be well-researched, thoughtful, easy to read and informative. It is an excellent "first" source for anyone considering the purchase of a franchise, or deciding whether to enter the arena to franchise their existing business. I am particularly impressed that the book is written in language that most people can understand. It covers the entire range of franchise-related subjects -- and would even be very useful for those simply starting their own business. Cited examples will be very helpful to all business newcomers."

Robert W. Ball, President and Founder
The Franchise Company
3472 Parkside Drive
San Bernardino, CA 92404
909-886-1261
909-882-8269 (fax)
www.franchising-consultants.com

THE
FRANCHISE
Handbook

A Complete Guide to All Aspects of BUYING, SELLING or INVESTING in a Franchise

The Franchise Handbook: A Complete Guide to All Aspects of Buying, Selling or Investing in a Franchise

Copyright © 2006 by Atlantic Publishing Group, Inc.

1210 SW 23rd Place • Ocala, Florida 34474 • 800-814-1132 • 352-622-5836–Fax

Web site: www.atlantic-pub.com • E-mail sales@atlantic-pub.com

SAN Number: 268-1250

ISBN-13: 978-0-910627-54-2

ISBN-10: 0-910627-54-1

Library of Congress Cataloging-in-Publication Data

The franchise handbook : a complete guide to all aspects of buying, selling or investing in a franchise.
    p. cm.
Includes index.
 ISBN 0-910627-54-1 (alk. paper)
 1. Franchises (Retail trade) I. Title.

HF5429.23.H38 2005
658.8'708--dc22

2005024706

ART DIRECTION, FRONT COVER & INTERIOR DESIGN: Meg Buchner • megadesn@mchsi.com

BOOK PRODUCTION DESIGN: Laura Siitari of Siitari by Design • www.siitaribydesign.com

Printed in the United States

TABLE OF CONTENTS

CHAPTER 4
ESTIMATING START-UP COSTS   57

CHAPTER 5
GETTING FINANCING   79

CHAPTER 6
CONDUCTING A MARKET ANALYSIS   89

CHAPTER 7
CREATING FINANCIAL STATEMENTS   99

CHAPTER 8
LOCATING YOUR FRANCHISE   115

CHAPTER 9
MARKETING YOUR FRANCHISE   123

CHAPTER 10
MANAGING EMPLOYEES 129

CHAPTER 11
BUYING AND MANAGING SUPPLIES 139

CHAPTER 12
MANAGING SUPPLIER AND FRANCHISER
RELATIONSHIPS 147

CHAPTER 13
COST CONTROL 161

CHAPTER 14
TERRITORIAL STRATEGIES 163

CHAPTER 15
EXPANDING YOUR OPERATIONS 169

CHAPTER 16
ADVANTAGES AND DISADVANTAGES OF THE
FRANCHISE MODEL 185

CHAPTER 17
FRANCHISING YOUR BUSINESS 195

CHAPTER 18
FRANCHISING AND THE LAW   221

CHAPTER 19
FRANCHISING RESOURCES   229

GLOSSARY   273

INDEX   287

FOREWORD

Do you dream of having the independence that being your own boss brings, the security that no one can fire you, enjoying a good income, and possibly, the accumulation of wealth and prosperity? Unfortunately, the cards are stacked against a new small business being successful or even making it at all. An endless stream of problems makes competition from large, sophisticated chains just too intense. Many new start-ups end as failures.

Franchising represents a different approach to business ownership. For an up-front fee plus ongoing royalties, the parent company teaches its business methods to the franchise-operator (franchisee) who bears all operating and financial responsibilities of the outlet. Some statistics are impressive: it is said more than 40 percent of all U.S. retail sales are through franchised establishments. While giants like McDonalds, H&R Block and Radio Shack are familiar, household names, franchises are available in a wide range of industries. The list of 3,000-plus franchise companies spans more than 100 different categories. But just as franchising represents a chance to get rich, it's also a chance to get stung. An alarming number of franchise operators make less than the minimum wage, working 60 to 80 hours a week, pursuing an expensive and elusive American dream that turns into a nightmare. Since the royalty payment comes right off the top, as a percentage of gross sales, the franchise companies get an assured revenue stream, even if franchised units are operating unprofitably and are sold over and over to new buyers.

For the last 25 years, as a franchise attorney, author, instructor and recognized expert, I've helped companies enter franchising – each hoping to become the next "McDonalds" of their respective industries. Along the way, I met and worked with an interesting group of entrepreneurial founders. From apparel to water treatment, the franchised concepts were incredibly diverse. Some of them interested me to the point where I considered buying a franchise myself. In two or three cases, I initiated talks to discuss the possibility but never moved forward. I just couldn't find the precise set of criteria to satisfy my exacting requirements in spite of having advised hundreds of prospective franchise buyers and developed sophisticated radar for detecting the good, the bad, and the ugly in franchising.

In 2002, my life changed dramatically as I took the leap and became a first-time franchise owner. It was in a niche of the home improvement industry never franchised before, and my wife and I bought their first franchise. Although this is not the recommended approach 99 percent of the time, I knew the principals and founder, so I was willing to take and manage the risk. Under the able assistance of the franchise company, we developed our franchise from scratch, leasing and improving a 7,000 square foot production warehouse and showroom. Gradually ramping up to our final crew of one part-time and three full-time employees, we settled on a Monday through Thursday 7 a.m. to 5 p.m. work week, so we had three-day weekends every weekend. Financially, we hit the critical break even point (where sales paid all operating expenses) in the sixth week of starting operations. Our total investment at that point was just under $100,000, including the initial $20,000 franchise and training fee.

When we sold our franchise in 2003 for $235,000 we were doing over $10,000 a week in sales with just a single crew, and our customers were on a six-to-eight week waiting list. Due to the size of our facility and nature of the interior door replacement business, three crews were planned. Bringing them online, one crew at a time, would double, then ultimately triple sales. In June 2003 we began interviewing a host of interested buyers. Sales were $47,000 less expenses of $35,500, leaving a profit that month of $11,500. You won't find this kind of track record or performance in 95 percent of the franchises out there. The challenge is to eliminate the 95 percent and concentrate on the 5 percent that truly deserve your evaluation efforts.

The American dream in franchising is still possible, but having a cautious attitude in evaluating franchise investments is never a bad thing. Take your time, evaluate many factors, and keep emotions out of the investment decision. If this is done you will avoid the three mistakes made by most first-time franchise buyers. Often this is easier said than done, especially when franchise companies use misleading success statistics to sell their franchises.

For example, if you come across a franchise company whose promotional materials claim franchises generally enjoy a 90 percent success rate, compared to less than 20 percent for independent firms, red flags should go up. The figures are based on unverified information supplied more than 20 years ago by a select, nonrepresentative group of franchise companies. A full third of the companies receiving "questionnaires " elected not to participate. Even more "studies" showing nine out of ten franchise owners consider their franchise to be somewhat or very successful also suffer from serious methodological flaws. These were simply telephone surveys of franchise owners who are asked to say (with absolutely no definition of the term "successful") whether they felt their business is "very unsuccessful," "somewhat unsuccessful," somewhat successful" or "very successful." I remember evaluating an existing pizza franchise for a client ten years ago. I asked the current owner if his business was successful. He said it was very successful. But his financial statements revealed he'd never taken a dollar out of the business for himself, the franchise never made a profit in two years of operation, and it was on the verge of bankruptcy. Particularly in franchising, "success" is a very subjective term.

In contrast, a study by Dr. Timothy Bates of more than 7000 firms was the first to compare start-up costs, profitability, and failure rates for franchised vs. nonfranchised firms. Published in the mid 1990s, Dr. Bates's study concluded, "Despite their larger revenues, much greater capitalization, and their supposed advantages of affiliation with a franchiser-parent firms, the franchisees lag behind cohort young firms in profitability and rates of survival." Not surprisingly, I'm not aware of a single franchise company that includes Dr Bates' study in their promotional materials.

This book has much to recommend it. The principal focus is devoted to the engaging topic of becoming a franchise owner. The last third of the book covers how firms enter the franchise industry—selling franchises as opposed to burgers or tax returns and etc. What makes the book interesting and informative is that it contains a wealth of knowledge and guidance not currently available in other franchise literature. It is useful to individuals considering franchise investments as well as professional advisors such as attorneys and accountants, so they can help clients make informed decisions. By following the advice provided, those interested in a franchise will have a path and process to follow. This will help ensure that the most important financial and emotional decision of your life is made from careful analysis and introspection — as opposed to blind faith and emotion. If you decide to invest in a franchise, the book contains many other useful chapters that will help you develop a business plan for obtaining a loan — something many franchise owners need but do not get — assistance from their franchise company. Finally, there is an entire section comprised of eight chapters devoted to running your franchise and managing the franchise relationship. These can be used as a "reality check" to verify you're receiving value in the franchise relationship, as well as additional information to maximize business performance.

Kevin B. Murphy, B.S., M.B.A., J.D.
Mr. Franchise
Franchise Foundations
San Francisco, CA

Kevin B. Murphy, referred to in the industry as "Mr. Franchise," is a nationally-known franchise attorney, author, university lecturer, and expert in franchising. For the past 25 years he has advised hundreds of franchise buyers as well as helped franchise companies enter the industry. Mr. Murphy has also owned and successfully operated a franchise in the home-improvement industry. Since 1990, he has been an approved provider for minimum continuing legal education, teaching franchise courses to attorneys. For more information, visit www.franchisefounda-tions.com or call 800-942-4402.

CHAPTER 1

Choosing the Right Franchise

You're interested in buying a franchise, but how do you know which franchise is right for you? Which franchise will suit your individual knowledge, skills, goals and preferred level of involvement? By choosing the right franchise, your chances of success increase substantially—most failed franchises result from a buyer not doing sufficient research to find the franchise that suits him best. This chapter will help you decide how to choose the perfect franchise and will tell you where to find the information essential to making your choice.

FRANCHISES ARE NOT INDEPENDENT BUSINESSES

The first thing any franchisee must realize is that a franchise is not an independent business. Franchising is not for you if you are the type of person who needs exacting control over your business. Do not forget: when you purchase a franchise, you are simply providing the capital to enable another person's dream, idea or product enter the marketplace. Why? Because it has already proven its worth—it works.

Most independent businesses fail within three years of their launch. A large amount of capital, time, energy, and personal sacrifice is needed to make an independent business succeed. Don't let this deter you, though, if you have a big, new idea for a product or service that you are sure consumers cannot live without—perhaps establishing an independent business is the way to go.

There are many resources available to help you decide whether your business idea is worth pursuing.

- Check out the **Service Corps of Retired Executives (SCORE) (www.score.org)**. The Corps partners with the U.S. Small Business Administration (SBA) (**www.sbaonline.sba.gov**) and offers the advice and counseling of retired business executives to those thinking about starting an independent business. SCORE can help with financial planning, creating and following a business plan, and other issues that are critical to starting a business.

- **The Small Business Development Center (SBDC) (www.sbaonline.sba.gov/sbdc)** is another organization affiliated with the SBA. The SBDC has 63 of its own centers across the nation, as well as more than 1100 offices within local schools, colleges, and chambers of commerce. Your local SBDC can provide you with technical and management assistance for your independent business.

Before establishing an independent business, you should do extensive market research on your idea. Is it appealing to consumers? Will it have a market? Have SCORE and an SBDC review your findings and point out any weaknesses. Also, be sure that your idea is economically feasible. Will your costs (rent, inventory, taxes, fees, payroll, insurance, legal fees) be covered by your revenue? Is your product pricing fair? Do you have a supportive and reliable bank? Once again, use SCORE and an SBDC to be sure your financial calculations make sense.

BECOMING A FRANCHISEE

Establishing an independent business may seem like a lot of work. It does hold a great amount of risk. If you do not have a unique product in mind and you want to build upon the proven success, reputation, and customer base of an established product or service, then franchising is your answer. Unlike in independent businesses, decisions are made for you by experienced industry professionals. Your name, trademark, and product line are known, trusted, and recognizable from day one.

If you decide to go this route, you still have a large and vastly important decision to make—which franchise is right for you? Which franchise will keep you interested, will make proper use of your skills and knowledge, and will bring you profit in the end? You have a number of options as you begin to gather the information that will enable you to choose exactly the right franchise.

You may have considered visiting a franchise broker. Brokers have low fees and can match you to a franchise based on your education, skills, and psychological attributes. However, you should know that brokers match you based upon a small list of available franchises. Brokers are paid by franchisers to market their businesses. That means that brokers will not suggest all possible options, but only those businesses with which they are in partnership. In order to find the perfect franchise, narrowing your options by visiting a broker is probably not your best bet.

We suggest gathering your own information to make the most informed choice. Don't worry! A number of resources exist that can help you. The most important thing to remember at the information-gathering stage is to remain organized. Keep organized and detailed records of names, databases, and Web sites. Be sure you record which information goes with which franchise or industry. Such detailed analyses will prove invaluable when the time comes to make your final selection.

Begin your information gathering by making a list of questions. When beginning a new enterprise, everyone has concerns and needs as well as more general questions. Write these questions down, and do not stop gathering information until you have a satisfactory answer to every one. Try to find the overlap in your questions and answers. How do the questions and answers interact? Such observations can provide you with even deeper insight.

What kinds of questions should you be asking? In addition to any personal needs or expectations, you should consider company and product longevity, competition, and modernization. For example, you should research the company's past financial records and its relationship with other companies. You should also research where the market and technology are heading and assess the company's products and services in that light. Has the company stayed up to date with current trends? Are there any upcoming introductions of new products or services that might threaten the company's own products and services? If so, how would the company be likely to respond? Is the company expanding? Is it focused? What kinds of services and support does it offer its franchisees? Finally, if your franchise would require employees other than yourself, is the labor attractive? Would you be able to offer competitive pay rates?

The answers to your questions can be found on the Internet, in franchise and business directories, in books and magazines, and at trade shows.

Internet

Much useful information can be found online. As with all Internet research, be careful of your sources. You should especially be sure to check the individual Web sites of the companies you are considering taking a franchise with.

Directories

A number of franchise directories are available to assist you. Directories are the best place to begin the information gathering process.

- **Franchise Opportunities Guide (www.franchise. org)**. Published bi-yearly by the International Franchise Association (IFA), this guide contains essential information such as the names and contact information of franchisers, suppliers, and legal consultants specializing in the franchise industry. It also includes franchise statistics and articles of interest to the franchisee. You can order the guide through the IFA at (800) 543-1038 or via the IFA Web site for $17.

- **Franchise Update Publications (www.franchise-update. com)**. This organization publishes a number of guides, including Executive's Guide to Franchise Opportunities; Food Service Guide to Franchise Opportunities; Guide to Multiple-Unit Franchise Opportunities; and Franchise Update Magazine. These are essential publications. For information about ordering them, go to the Web site or call (800) 289-4232.

- **Bond's Franchise Guide (www.worldfranchising.com)**. This guide covers both the United States and Canada and includes contact information for more than 1000 franchisers. It costs $29.95 and can be purchased at (800) 841-0873 or via the Web site. World Franchising also publishes a number of helpful books.

- **Franchise Annual (www.infonews.com)**. This guide also publishes franchiser contact information, along with brief business descriptions and fees. The guide is available online and can be purchased for $44.95 by calling (716) 754-4669 or via the Info News Web site.

- **Franchise Handbook (www.franchisel.com).** This handbook is published quarterly and contains information about companies offering current franchise opportunities. The handbook also contains relevant articles and success stories. The handbook is issued quarterly and you can subscribe to it for $29.95 a year at (800) 272-0246 or via the Web site.

- **International Herald Tribune International Franchise Guide (www.franchiseintl.com).** This annual publication, printed by Source Book Publications, contains information on international franchising. It can be purchased for $29.95 at (510) 839-5471 or from the Web site.

Consumer Business Publications

There are a number of business publications and newspapers you should consult for information that is useful to the future and current franchisee:

- *Inc.* (**www.inc.com**)

- *Entrepreneur* (**www.entrepreneurmag.com**)

- *Franchise Times* (**www.franchisetimes.com**)

- *Franchising World* (**www.franchise.org**)

- *Franchise Update* (**www.franchise-update.com**)

- *USA Today* (**www.usatoday.com**)

- *The Wall Street Journal* (**www.wsj.com**)

- *The New York Times* (**www.nytimes.com**)

Trade Shows and Expositions

Franchise trade shows may be the best source for information. Most importantly, they offer the opportunity to meet face to face with prospective franchisers. You should leave a trade show with brochures, pamphlets, and other great tools for answering the questions you wrote down at the beginning of the information-gathering stage.

The world's largest trade show, the International Franchise Expo, is sponsored by the IFA and is held annually in Washington, D.C. This gathering includes hundreds of organizations offering franchises to interested individuals and includes classes for an extra fee. It is well worth a visit. Information can be obtained from the IFA at 1501 K Street NW, Suite 350, Washington, D.C. 20005, **www.franchise.org**, or (202) 628-8000.

Additional smaller shows are held every year. For starters, your local SBDC might hold low-fee seminars of interest to you. In addition, regional trade shows are held throughout the year and could include franchise opportunities specific to the needs and market of your home region. Check the Internet for these.

Keep the following things in mind when visiting a trade show.

- **Make sure you are dealing with a franchise** and not some other kind of business opportunity. Many companies at trade shows offer "multi-level marketing plans" or other such business plans. These are not franchises. The best way to ensure that you are looking at a true franchise is to ask for a copy of the company's Uniform Franchise Offering Circular, or UFOC. These circulars, which must conform to FTC regulations, ensure that the company is offering a true franchise. They contain a wealth of relevant and important information about the franchise opportunity. (More information on UFOCs is provided in Chapter 3). You may be asked to sign for the circular and to provide your contact information. This is acceptable. Taking a UFOC and reviewing it does not mean you are under any obligation to buy a franchise. Companies are required to abide by a ten-day "cooling off period" before selling a franchise, giving the prospective franchisee and franchiser time to reconsider and clear up any mistakes. By providing your contact information, the company can ensure that you purchase your franchise legally. Franchises cannot be purchased legally at a trade show.

- **Have a plan before you walk into the trade show.**
  Take the time to look at the show directory before the event, and know which franchises you want to examine. Structure and organization are your most important allies. Have any specific questions about your chosen franchises ready beforehand.

BUYING AN EXISTING FRANCHISE

After you've done your research and determined which franchise is right for you, you need to consider some additional issues. One of the most important is: should you build a new location, or should you purchase an existing location from another franchisee? This section explores the latter option.

Often, companies provide a list of existing franchise locations that are available either from a current franchisee or from the company directly. Such locations provide the benefit of being already established, with a presence in the community and an existing customer base. In addition, these locations often already have trained employees, and many may be willing to stay through the change in management. Taking over such a location can save you months of preparation and allow you to bypass such time-consuming steps as finding an appropriate location, negotiating a lease, and hiring.

Before you purchase an existing location, be sure to research its history. Some owners might be planning a retirement, looking for a new occupation, or have other such innocuous reasons for "getting out." However, it's also possible that the location is suffering, and the owner is looking to "unload" on another buyer. Do not count on the existing owner to provide you with all the information you need to make an educated choice. Rather, use all the resources at your disposal to discover what you need to know about a location's history. Check media sources, public records, and available financial data. Is the owner legally obligated to share any franchise information? If so, it would be good information to have and useful to the reader.

If you find that a location's history is not favorable, you need to be able to determine the cause of any failures. Sometimes, a new owner with energy and foresight is all that is needed to bring new life to a beleaguered franchise. However, location problems, competition problems, or other such issues may be less easily overcome.

Purchasing an existing franchise will undoubtedly cut down on advertising, hiring, and other costs associated with opening a new location. However, you will most likely have to pay a transfer fee (a fixed fee or a percentage), in addition to some legal fees. Also, be sure to pay close attention to the terms of the new franchise contract. Some owners may sell you only the remainder of their own contract rather than a new, full-term contract.

If you are interested in finding existing franchises that are up for sale, take a look at the Business Resale Network Web site: **www.br-network.com**.

STARTING NEW

If you would rather purchase a franchise and open a new location, odds are that you will not be entirely on your own. However, the help you might receive in this endeavor will vary from company to company. While the franchiser will often help you to locate an appropriate property, sign a lease, advertise, and hire help, be sure of the quality of the assistance you can expect to receive before agreeing to the purchase.

Getting to know the franchiser and other of its franchisees in person is a good step to take in deciding if the franchiser will provide you with the aid you might need as you begin your business venture. Take a trip to company headquarters—it is well worth the expense. Talk to the staff, evaluate the premises, and decide if the company is well run. If it is not well-run, and if there are disgruntled staff members at headquarters, chances are that franchisees are also unhappy. Take any invitations to tour premises and other outlets, but also take the initiative to visit some outlets unexpectedly. If you are touring with other interested franchisees, make yourself known and share information.

Likewise, ask current owners of the franchise if they have received satisfactory aid from the parent company. While you're at it, ask about any problems they have encountered and how the problems were solved, how much capital was required for them to set up their franchise and how long it took for them to begin realizing a profit.

Just as you should get to know the company on a personal level, you should expect a quality company to want to get to know you as well. Good, responsible companies will only want to sell franchises to responsible franchisees. If a company takes your check without any kind of interviewing or examination of your background, how interested are they in the success of their company, and how interested will they be in you and your personal success after that check is cashed?

If you find yourself satisfied with the company and how it is run and if you are confident that the company will provide you with the startup help you will need, begin to search for the right site to establish your new location. You should consider such things as demographics, traffic patterns, crime, zoning, future construction projects (contact your local zoning board for this kind of information), and competition in the immediate area. It might be helpful to interview pedestrians or other local business owners to get an idea if your franchise would be welcome and successful in the neighborhood.

Stay organized, stay focused, and use all the resources available to you. Choose the right franchise and take intelligent initial steps, and your chances of success will increase dramatically.

COMPANY: Candy Bouquet International

Margaret McEntire is the Owner/Founder of Candy Bouquet International. Candy Bouquet International is the largest candy franchise in the world with more than 750 stores in more than 40 countries; Margaret McEntire believes that being innovative and creative is the best way to keep her franchise on top.

"My idea was unique and no one had ever franchised an idea like it before. I threw out the book on what anyone else was doing and tried to do what was right for my business. I had to grow with the business as well. I see new programs that implement it. New franchise ideas are always brewing and we are in a constant 'mode of change.' Nothing is ever written in stone. We are nothing but an innovative group, re-inventing each day with new ideas and future plans."

CHAPTER

2 Doing Your Research

When it comes time for the nitty gritty of research, organization and preparedness are key. You will be inundated with material during your search for information. This chapter will help you to tackle the stacks of paper you are likely to collect.

INTERNET RESEARCH

The Internet is beneficial in that it allows companies and individuals to publish and disseminate information freely. However, this open use can also be a hindrance because the quality of information on the Internet varies widely. Despite this, the Internet is probably going to be your primary tool as you collect preliminary and background information.

If you were to go to "Google" and enter the word "franchise," you would find more than 60 million results. Internet research is most useful if you focus your search on companies, products, or services in which have an interest. Focus your attention on these companies or products, and try to ignore the bogus advertisements and other schemes meant to redirect your attention to less legitimate enterprises. The Internet is only a starting point, a means to gather contact numbers and general information. In the end, you will need to make phone calls, attend interviews, and otherwise "get out there" to gather information to make an intelligent decision.

SEPARATE THE GOOD, THE BAD, AND THE UGLY

For effective Internet research results, you need to learn how to sort the useful from the worthless. It is helpful to be on the lookout for certain characteristics that are very common among untrustworthy or illegitimate franchising sites. This section will give you some useful tips.

- **Look for disclosure information.** While many companies will provide UFOCs in electronic versions on the Internet, you should be aware that the federal government has yet to make these electronic versions legal. A franchiser who delivers these documents in electronic form is not abiding by FTC regulations, and should probably not be trusted. However, if a Web site with such UFOCs provides a disclaimer stating that electronic documents cannot be used to buy or sell a franchise, you can be more confident that the company is legitimate and trustworthy.

- **Check for the quality of grammar and spelling on a site.** Poor spelling and grammar are very often a sign that something is amiss. Highly professional, legitimate companies will post only well-written information on their Web sites.

- **Avoid doing business with companies that have "hype" on their sites.** A good company can sell itself with facts, figures, and other concrete indications of success. A company that tries to sell itself with overblown statements and self-accolades most likely simply has nothing more substantial to say.

- **Avoid sites with overly aggressive marketing.** As in the previous tip, a truly successful company will be able to sell itself with facts rather than aggressive sales tactics or intimidation.

- **Avoid dealing with a company that does not provide full financial details at the outset.** You should be able to browse estimated setup costs, fees, cash flows, and other such financial information freely. Companies that hide this information probably have even more to hide.

STARTING POINTS

We would like to recommend a few starting points to those who have no idea where to begin. While our list is in no way exhaustive, it contains great sites with trustworthy information.

Franchises are heavily regulated by state and national governments, so governmental Web sites often contain a large amount of useful and trustworthy information. We suggest you begin with the Federal Trade Commission (**www.ftc.gov**). The FTC plays a large part in the regulation of franchises, and disseminates a great deal of information for franchisees. Here you can find laws, legal actions, investigations, and proceedings against faulty franchisers.

We also recommend the following sites: *Entrepreneur* magazine at **www.entrepreneurmag.com; www.franchise.com**; the IFA at **www.franchise.org; www.franchisesolutions.com;** and **www. franchiseopportunties.com**.

STAYING ORGANIZED

Like most people, you will probably want to print out the information you find on the Internet, and after your Internet research, when you visit franchise expositions and begin to correspond with companies, you will probably get a massive amount of printed material to organize. Rather than creating slipshod piles around your home or office, you will be best served by systematically organizing your materials.

Prepare to organize your materials even before you begin collecting them. Visit your local office supply store and purchase an affordable filing system, along with hanging folders, tab folders, and labels. As you begin to gather information, create a separate file folder for each company you correspond with or consider corresponding with. Within each company folder, create subfolders for such categories as correspondence (letters sent and received, contact information, memos, faxes, and business cards); promotional items (brochures, glossies, and other printed information); legal items (UFOCs and contracts); and operational items. This last category, which will come into play once you've made a deal with a franchiser, will include items concerning operational specifics such as potential locations, suppliers, and employees. Additional categories can be created according to your own needs, but the above categories (at minimum) are suggested for careful organization of your materials. Such a filing system will be a great help as you attempt to locate specific information quickly and successfully.

Even after you have purchased a franchise, keep the information you have filed. You can never tell what might happen in the future and having your self-created database at your fingertips will be a blessing should you change your mind about your purchase.

CHAPTER

3

Signing on the Dotted Line: Legal Issues

Franchising became popular in the 1950s, when scores of World War II veterans came home and found excess money stuffing their pockets due to the GI Bill and other financial provisions. By the 1960s it became apparent that unregulated franchising led to many problems for franchisees. Spurred on by the franchising craze, many franchisers were more interested in selling franchises and than they were making sure that the franchises they sold were sound and successful. In response, state and federal governments made the first attempts at regulation, and in 1979 the FTC implemented a minimum disclosure rule.

Franchisers are now required to comply with laws stipulating the creation of a Uniform Franchise Offering Circular (UFOC), which communicates to potential franchisees basic information about the individual franchise system. The UFOC will be discussed in more detail in the following section; for now, it is important to know that while it is required for the sale of a franchise, this document does not need federal approval. However, state approval of the document is required in 14 states: California, Hawaii, Illinois, Indiana, Maryland, Michigan, Minnesota, New

York, North Dakota, Rhode Island, South Dakota, Virginia, Washington, and Wisconsin. In other states, state approval of the UFOC is not required, but the franchiser must register its intent to sell franchises within state territory. Those states are: Florida, Kentucky, Nebraska, Texas, and Utah. Many states have additional laws, called "relationship laws," which ensure that a franchiser cannot terminate a contract or refuse to renew an agreement at the end of its term without substantial reason. More information on termination is contained in Chapter 18.

UNDERSTANDING THE UFOC

The FTC requires the creation of a UFOC for all franchises, the North American Securities Administrators Association (NASAA) has created guidelines dictating the kind of information that should be contained in a UFOC, including information about the franchiser and the franchise system, and the relationship the franchisee should expect to have with the franchiser. The FTC accepts the NASAA guidelines as sufficient, and most franchisers use the NASAA format when creating the document.

Here is what franchisees should expect to find in a UFOC: management history and experience; contact and background information for key staff; financial history; legal history; and fee schedules pertaining to opening, running, and closing the franchise. Information about existing franchises should also be provided, including the number of existing franchises and the number opened, closed, and transferred. Additionally, a franchisee should expect to find information on projected capital investment, required purchases, and territorial rights, if applicable. Finally, a franchisee should be notified of relationship requirements and mutual expectations.

As mentioned in the previous chapter, the UFOC is governed by a 10-day cooling off period, dubbed the "10-day rule." Once a potential franchisee has the UFOC, a franchiser must wait a minimum of 10 days before accepting an offer to buy. Often, the UFOC in its raw form will contain blanks to be filled in, for instance, location and definition of territory. Any such changes made to the UFOC will cause a five-day waiting period to kick in. The 10-day and five-day waiting periods *can* run at the same time. In other words, you don't have to wait 15 days.

A UFOC has 23 required sections, which are explained below. Pay particular attention to items 7, 17, and 19.

- **Item 1.** This section goes into historical detail about the franchiser and discusses its predecessors, if any. It also contains contact information, information on trade names, and information on the franchiser's experience in the business.

- **Item 2.** In this section you will find the names and experience of any big players in the franchise program.

- **Item 3.** Litigation history is provided in this section. Any litigation in which the franchiser was involved that could have a potential impact on franchisees must be revealed.

- **Item 4.** A history of bankruptcy is given here. Any

bankruptcy filing in the past 15 years must be disclosed, including bankruptcies filed by leading officers of the franchise program.

- **Item 5.** The initial fee and/or payment expected from the franchisee is provided in this section. Terms of payment and refund policies are also discussed.

- **Item 6.** Other fees are revealed here, including those for advertising, royalties, insurance, training costs, accounting costs, leases, and so on.

- **Item 7.** Look here to determine what you can expect as an initial investment. This value might be an average or even an estimate, so use the contact information of other franchises provided in the UFOC to double-check this figure. Call the other franchisees and ask them what their initial investments were. In addition, compare the estimate in the UFOC to the market in your specific area. For example, rent estimates might differ widely from what you can actually expect to pay in rent.

- **Item 8.** This section outlines any obligations on the part of the franchisee to lease or purchase a location, goods, or services from particular, given sources. If the franchiser realizes financial gain from such obligations, this must be disclosed.

- **Item 9.** This section outlines any obligations on the part of the franchisee to lease or purchase a location, goods, or services from an approved supplier. Methods of gaining supplier approval are provided.

- **Item 10.** If any financing programs are offered by the franchiser, you will find a description of them here.

- **Item 11.** This section outlines any obligations on the part of the franchisee to employ certain services or assistance.

- **Item 12.** If you will be given exclusive rights to a territory, terms are provided here. If you are required to meet certain conditions to attain or maintain such rights, the conditions will be spelled out here.

- **Item 13.** Information concerning any legal trademarks, service marks, trade names, commercial symbols, and logos will be provided in this section.

- **Item 14.** Information concerning any copyrights or patents will be provided here.

- **Item 15.** If you are obligated to participate personally in your franchise your duties will be stated and outlined in this section.

- **Item 16.** If certain goods or services are not permitted to be offered by a franchisee, these will be mentioned in this section.

- **Item 17.** This is the "boilerplate" section of the UFOC, the fine print. **Read it.** It contains information on agreement renewal, transfer, and termination, as well as procedures used in case of a dispute. You need to know what will happen if a disagreement arises between you and the franchiser. This section might also contain noncompete agreements, which are important should you ever decide to terminate your franchise agreement.

- **Item 18.** Any endorsements or contracts with public figures will be revealed and discussed in this section. In addition, if any public figure owns or manages a part of the franchise program, franchisees must be informed here.

- **Item 19.** This is the earnings claim provided by the franchiser. In other words, this is where the franchiser tells you how much you can expect to make. (1) If this information is *not* provided, it is important that you estimate it yourself. Begin by asking other franchisees. You can also get an idea of earning potential by checking SEC reports (if the franchiser is a publicly traded company). In addition, try checking the Internet. Using a variety of sources, including other information contained in the UFOC, you can arrive at an approximate expectation of earnings. (2) If this information *is* in the UFOC, keep in mind that the franchiser can also legally provide you with a figure that differs from the one in the UFOC and that will be more in line with earnings expectations for your particular region or circumstances. This must be provided in writing, along with an explanation of why it differs from the figure provided in the UFOC, and a copy must be provided to the franchisee. Do not accept an oral earnings claim; insist upon a paper document.

Robert Bond has published a collection of earnings claims included by franchisers in their UFOCs. The book is called *How Much Can I Make?* and it retails for $29.95. To order, call (800) 841-0873 or visit **www.worldfranchising. com**.

- **Item 20.** In this section you will find a list of all operating franchises in the system; any franchises that have been shut down; the number of new franchise agreements made; and any company-owned franchises.

- **Item 21.** A complete set of financial statements is provided in this section. For example, the franchiser might provide a balance sheet for the previous year, an income statement, and documentation of changes in financial position in the past three years. Many states require that these statements be audited.

- **Item 22.** A copy of any forms required to be signed by the franchisee upon purchase are included in this section, including a copy of the franchise agreement.

- **Item 23.** The last item of a UFOC is a receipt acknowledging the reception of the UFOC by a potential franchisee.

Understanding the Federal Trade Commission Cover Sheet

This document will contain the franchiser's name and location, a date of issuance, and a statement from the FTC emphasizing that the information contained in the UFOC has not been checked by federal agents for accuracy and that the government has not officially approved the UFOC. Remember, the government has never officially approved any UFOC.

Understanding the State Registration Page

A state registration page will only be included with UFOCs drawn up in states requiring the registration of franchises. It will include the franchiser's trademark, logo, or other symbol under which the franchiser operates (this symbol should be owned outright by the franchiser), a description of the business, and complete contact information for the franchiser. Additionally, the state registration page will contain information on the amount a franchisee can expect to invest for his or her initial purchase along with risk factors that the franchisee should consider. You should show these risk factors to your attorney. Also, be sure to contact the FTC to inquire about the franchiser; you might be provided with additional information—such as any complaints filed against the franchiser—that will influence your decision. Remember that registration with the state does not guarantee the quality of the franchise. Even low-quality franchisers must register.

Understanding and Negotiating the Franchise Agreement

The agreement you will have to sign after you actually purchase a franchise is different from the UFOC. While the UFOC describes a franchiser, a franchise, and the relationship between the franchiser and franchisee, the franchise agreement is a legally binding contract that governs these relations. It is important that you review the contract and understand it thoroughly. You may want to acquire the services of a franchise attorney to help you navigate the document and to answer any questions you might have about legal matters and obligations.

The uniformity of the franchise system makes the system effective, but it can also be a source of contention between you and your franchiser. A franchise agreement spells out the specific requirements and conditions under which you are expected to operate your business. These conditions often conflict with your personal interests because they tend to favor the franchiser. Even so, uniformity is beneficial to you because it provides you with an established framework that is proven successful in the marketplace; after all, why else are you purchasing a franchise?

You do not need to accept unfair conditions. Your franchiser will always be the "boss," but that does not mean that you have to accept conditions which will provide the franchiser with all the benefits. Negotiation is possible to a limited extent. While a franchiser by law cannot treat units differently, some amount of negotiation is possible. The results will not change the basic uniformity of the agreement, but might help it to serve your interests better. Most franchisees do not negotiate because they do not know why, when, or how to do so. Usually established franchisers do not need to deal with negotiations as there are plenty of prospective franchisees ready to sign on, whatever the terms. With new franchise systems, though, franchisers are often willing to negotiate to get their systems up and running.

You should understand all the provisions in your franchise agreement and review the agreement with an attorney knowledgeable about franchise law. You should attempt to negotiate any points you believe are unfair or biased in the franchiser's favor. As with the UFOC, read the fine print in your franchise agreement. **You should know and understand every word in your franchise agreement before you sign it.**

Your review should not be rushed. Remember, the 10-day rule applies to the signing of any franchise agreement. It will take time for you to locate a qualified attorney and have him or her review and translate the document into terms you can understand. If there are any problems or points of needed negotiation, communicating with your franchiser will take time also. In any case, winning negotiations is uncommon — most franchisees walk away with a signed, standard franchise agreement — but there is no harm in trying!

HIRING A FRANCHISE LAWYER

Finding and retaining a lawyer is important. Not only will a lawyer help you to interpret the UFOC and franchise agreement contract, but he or she will also ensure that you do not inadvertently make any costly mistakes. He or she will be an invaluable member of your business team.

Be sure that you hire someone with expertise in franchise law. Franchise law is a specialty, just like import/export, personal injury, or patent law. A number of resources exist that can help you locate the right lawyer. Ask your personal lawyer, personal or professional acquaintances, or use the databases of the American Bar Association or the IFA. The American Bar Association hosts a forum dealing exclusively with franchising (**www.abnet.org**), which is organized according to geographic region. You can also purchase a directory for $35. As an alternative, obtain a copy of the *Franchise Opportunity Guide*, published by the Council of Franchise Suppliers of the IFA (**www.franchise.org**). The guide can be accessed online and contains a list of firms with specialists in franchise law. Finally, consider consulting the online Directory of Franchise Attorneys at **www.franchise-update.com**.

HIRING A FINANCIAL AND BUSINESS ADVISOR

It is in your best interest to acquire the services of a financial advisor. Tax and financial laws are complex, and finding a reliable banker, CPA, or CA will be a key to your success. Be sure you feel comfortable enough with your financial advisor to share personal and detailed information about your finances. You can locate a financial advisor through local association Web sites.

WHAT IS THE BEST WAY TO OWN AND OPERATE MY PARTICULAR BUSINESS?

In most cases, you will not own your business in your personal name, thus avoiding financial and legal obligations. Rather, you will want to form a business entity to own and operate the business. You have a number of choices, and selecting the one that will work best for you is important. The entity you choose can affect everything from your payment of taxes, liability, and financing options, as well as the kinds of relationships that will be fostered between you and your managers. While there are no guarantees, choosing the right entity to own your business will significantly decrease your chances of failure.

There are many legal forms from which you can choose, including a sole proprietorship, general or limited partnerships; a joint venture; a C or S corporation (depending upon other sources of income); a limited liability company; and a registered limited liability partnership. All of these options have their own advantages and disadvantages. Choosing the right one for you will largely depend upon your own goals and upon the functioning and structure of your particular business.

We recommend employing the services of a qualified attorney and accountant, both of whom should know a great deal about tax law and business operations. These professionals will be able to take you through potential business scenarios to help you determine which will work best with your business. They will also explain the tax implications of each entity.

PARTNERSHIPS: THE PROS AND CONS

This section will offer some words of advice on forming partnerships. These entities are frequently formed because friends and family, trusted and known, can be great sources of capital for a new venture. However, without the experience and aid of a qualified professional, the terms drawn up in a partnership can often lead to confusion, frustration, and even conflict between partners. This can be especially damaging if your partner is a close friend or family member. You want to avoid having your business affect your personal relationships at all costs.

For starters, you and your partner should consider each of the following points.

- Any initial investment will probably not be recouped within the first five years. It will take time for the business to realize a profit.

- Partnerships should never be divided 50-50. One partner should always hold a larger share, or else disagreement will lead to decisions never being made and necessary changes never being implemented.

- Divide time and duties between the partners beforehand.

- Think together about any other financial obligations likely to arise.

- Decide on a course of action should one partner choose to leave the partnership. You should both decide how to determine the value of the business at that point and any methods of compensation.

- Determine how the business will be divided upon

the death of one partner. Will the deceased's share be inherited by a relative, and if so, will the relative have the same control over the business as the deceased? If not, will the business simply pass in its entirety to the surviving partner, or will it transform into a different kind of entity?

Go over each of the above points with an attorney, and work through any disagreements. If you cannot agree on most of the above points, perhaps a partnership is not a good idea.

BUSINESS ENTITY COMPARISON CHART

Issue	Sole Proprietorship	General Partnership	Limited Partnership
Number of owners	One	Unlimited (at least two)	Unlimited, must have at least one general partner and one limited partner
Liability	Unlimited personal liability	Joint and several unlimited personal liability	Limited liability only if limited partners do not participate in management; unlimited liability for general partner
Federal income tax	Taxed at individual level	No tax at partnership level	No tax at limited partnership level
Management	By sole proprietor	By all partners	By general partners only to prevent limited partners from losing limited liability
Transferability of interest	Unrestricted— sale or transfer of business assets	Determined by partnership agreement	Determined by limited partnership agreement
Duration	As long as proprietor lives and operates	Indefinite, but may have to terminate earlier on occurrence of certain events (death, bankruptcy) to qualify as partnership for tax purposes	Indefinite, but may have to terminate earlier on occurrence of certain events (death, bankruptcy of a general partner) to qualify as partnership for tax purposes

BUSINESS ENTITY COMPARISON CHART (Continued)

Issue	Joint Venture	"C" Corporation	"S" Corporation
Number of owners	Unlimited (at least two)	Unlimited	Up to 75 individuals; no corporate, trust (with certain exceptions), or nonresident alien shareholders
Liability	Joint and several unlimited personal liability	Limited liability for shareholders even with shareholder participation in management	Limited liability for shareholders even with shareholder participation in management
Federal Income Tax	No tax at partnership level by joint venturers	Taxed on both corporate and shareholder level (double taxation)	Generally not taxed at the corporate level
Management	Determined by joint venture agreement	By board of directors or shareholders	By board of directors or shareholders
Transferability of interests		No restriction but subject to securities law and shareholders' agreement	No restriction but subject to securities law and shareholders' agreement
Duration	Indefinite, but may have to terminate earlier on occurrence of certain events (death, bankruptcy) to qualify as partnership for tax purposes	Perpetual	Perpetual

BUSINESS ENTITY COMPARISON CHART (Continued)

Issue	Limited Liability Company	"C" Corporation
Number of owners	Unlimited (but at least two in certain states)	Unlimited (but at least two)
Liability	Limited liability for members even with their management participation	No personal liability of partners for debts of the partnership or the malfeasance or malpractice of other partners
Federal income taxes	Not taxed at the company level; taxed as a partnership (no entity level of taxation)	Not taxed at the partnership level
Management	By member or a manager	By all partners
Transferability of interest	By statute other members must consent or no right to participate in management	Determined by limited liability partnership agreement
Duration	Maximum of 30 years, but may have to terminate earlier on occurrence of certain events in order to quality as partnership for tax purposes	Indefinite, but may have to terminate earlier on occurrence of certain events (death, bankruptcy) to quality as partnership for tax purposes

FORMING A BUSINESS ENTITY

Upon determining the entity under which you will operate, it is of vital importance that you comply with all laws pertaining to the operation of such an entity. You will need to perform all tasks and file all paperwork and records necessary to operate legally within the framework of that entity. Not doing so will negate your operating under an entity at all. In other words, by not following all bylaws and requirements, all protections gained by operating under a different entity will be lost.

You will need to follow all laws relating to the operation of your chosen entity type, including keeping current records, which should be signed by your attorney or accountant; filing all necessary tax documents on time; and signing any contracts using your entity title, for example, "president." Other tasks may apply. You should follow the guidance of your legal and financial representatives.

What Should I Do if I Already Own My Franchise Personally?

If you have already purchased your franchise in your own name, you need to transfer it to an entity. Most franchisers will allow you to do so as long as you remain personally obligated to the franchiser for the entity's obligations. The franchiser will want you to have the protections that owning under another entity will offer and will usually cooperate with your efforts to transfer. However, the franchiser might detail some conditions under which the transfer must take place. These conditions are usually listed in the franchise agreement and may include the following:

- You must remain the controlling party of the entity.

- The entity must be formed for the sole purpose of running the franchise.

- The entity cannot use any trade names associated with the franchise as part of its own name.

- The entity must state explicitly that it covers any and all obligations laid out in the franchise agreement.

- Any stock issued must contain information on restrictions put in place by the franchise agreement.

Using a Fictitious Name or Assumed Name Registration

In many states, you will be required by law to register your business along with your name and contact information so that anyone who would like to determine the owner of your business can do so. If you are a sole proprietor and use your full name as part of your business name, you will probably not need to worry about registration. In the same way, if you operate your business under a name identical to the name of your entity, then your entity name will already be registered, and registering the business separately will probably not be required. In any other case, you will need to follow the laws established by your state regarding fictitious names, trade names, and assumed names. You should inquire with your legal representative about any laws concerning this matter.

CHAPTER

Estimating Start-up Costs

This chapter will outline how to assess your personal financial situation and how to approach writing a business plan—an essential document for any business, independent or franchise. Start-up costs can be high, and unless you are positive of your ability to support yourself, your family, and your business, you should put off buying a franchise until you are ready to do so. Remember, you must have the money to support yourself and family for the first year or two of your business, in addition to what it is going to cost to purchase and open your franchise. The SBA and other experts agree that the primary cause of failed franchises is insufficient start-up capital.

Before you decide whether to purchase a franchise, the following questions are important. If you fall short in one or more areas, do not ignore the shortcoming, and do not attempt to compensate for it in other ways. Rather, consider what areas you might need help and if obtaining help is an option. You want to be honest with yourself and your ability to finance your venture. Do you have the means at this time to purchase a franchise?

The questions you must ask yourself are:

- How much cash do I have? ("Liquid" means something that can be sold for cash fairly easily.)

- What liquid investments do I have?

- Can I get equity from my home? Am I willing and able to take out a second mortgage?

- How many of my assets am I willing or able to lose?

- Should I partner, and if so, can the business support both me and my partner?

- What financing options do I have?

- Are friends and family willing to help me financially?

- Do I have a good credit rating?

- Do I have a good relationship with my bank?

- What land expenses will I face? Can I lease, or must I buy?

- Will the franchiser provide me with financing options?

Remember: opening a franchise can be less expensive in some ways than opening an independent business. You can rely on the franchiser in many cases to provide or endorse vendors, equipment, and other supplies needed to open your franchise. Also, your franchiser should provide you with a ballpark estimate of opening costs, and you have the experience and advice of other franchisees at your fingertips. These factors make assessing your financial readiness much easier than if you were opening an independent business.

START-UP COSTS

This section will provide you with an outline of the types of costs you need to take into consideration when thinking about start-up financing.

- **Franchise fees.** When you purchase a franchise, the franchiser will most likely charge you fees for any start-up assistance. This assistance will aid you with many of the tasks listed below, such as location selection, advertising, and support during your first few months. In very rare cases you will be provided this kind of aid at no cost, but typically you can expect to pay between $20,000 and $25,000. (Some franchise fees are in excess of $100,000.)

- **Finding the right location for your business.** Before you choose an appropriate location, you need to put some time and money into researching factors like demographics, traffic, crime, and local competition. You should also consider personal travel time and expenses.

The more locations you research, the more money you can expect to spend. Research as many locations as possible; finding the ideal location for your business is well worth the cost.

- **Property expenses.** Once you've chosen your location, you will need to decide whether to buy or rent. Renting will require a deposit. And whether you buy or lease, expect to pay for utilities.

- **Zoning expenses.** If your ideal location is not zoned for your business type, you will need to petition the zoning board to allow an exception. This will cost fees (and time).

- **Contractor expenses.** Once you're zoned and ready to build, you'll need to hire a contractor. Even if the franchiser has provided you with architectural plans, you will possibly need to hire an architect to revise those plans to suit your specific location. You will need to develop and maintain a bid book and equipment lists, and don't forget to factor in landscaping and appliance costs.

- **Décor expenses.** You're built and ready to decorate. While your building may have been largely pre-designed by the franchiser, you still need to add your own finishing touches. What about pictures for the walls? What lighting do you need?

- **Inventory expenses.** You are ready to stock your location for business. You will need to purchase any ingredients or materials needed to create saleable items. Don't forget, making your opening inventory purchase means filling your store with saleable goods from nothing. You will also have to buy janitorial items, clerical equipment for the office, and other items. Do not forget to factor in shipping costs and sales taxes.

- **Insurance expenses.** You have a newly built store stocked full of items. It is absolutely vital that you purchase good insurance. You will need insurance against theft, vandalism, and acts of nature, as well as insurance against injury and death for customers and employees. Depending on your business, you might need auto insurance or other more industry-specific insurance. Plan to pay the entire premium up front, although you may be able to get away with a deposit.

- **Pre-opening labor expenses.** Finally, you are ready to start business. What about employees? It will take time and money to locate and hire the right group of people. After they are hired, they will also need to be trained. Some franchisers offer special training workshops for employees of their franchisees; you, as the franchisee, will be responsible for paying their wages during training. You must also consider the income you will lose while attending training yourself and any travel expenses for yourself or for your employees.

- **Professional fees.** As discussed in the previous chapter, you will need to retain a lawyer and accountant to ensure accurate legal and financial records. These fees can add up quickly.

- **Promotional expenses.** Now, you're ready for business. Time to let the public know you exist! Don't forget—it is your responsibility to use your own talent and enterprise to promote your business.

The bottom line is, you can expect to shell out $100,000 to $300,000 in start-up costs. Sometimes this figure will be as high as $1 million. Start-up costs will depend, of course, on your franchise; you should receive an estimated figure in your circular. Don't forget that you will need working capital to supplement your revenue in the beginning, sometimes for up to two years. Consult an accountant for estimates on this cost. Franchisers will often expect you to invest from 35 to 50 percent of the estimated start-up cost to ensure that you have the funds to successfully begin your business.

In general, Internet- or vehicle-based businesses are less expensive to start up than brick and mortar businesses.

RAISING THE MONEY TO START

Now that you have some idea of your own personal financial situation and of the start-up costs you can expect, you should begin to determine where you fall short and what you can do to raise the funds you need. While you will depend largely upon your own savings, equity, and loans from banks and associates, you might also be able to obtain financial assistance from your franchiser. Some franchisers might offer deferred payment programs, training expenses, supplier financing, or profit-sharing programs. Also, ask if buildings or land are available to lease directly from the franchiser or if a joint venture is possible. If you are a corporate employee of the franchiser, they might offer you reduced franchise fees. This works in their favor as well because they are selling a franchise to someone already familiar with the business.

Loans can sometimes be obtained directly from the franchiser, or alternatively, the franchiser may nurture relationships with loaners willing to aid qualified franchisees or they may guarantee the loan for a bank. The Franchise Registry, maintained by the SBA, lists companies with franchises that are pre-approved for expedited loans (**www.franchiseregistry.com**).

Bank loans are another option. Even if you do not borrow money from a bank, be sure you have a bank with experience in small business banking and with which you have a good, established relationship. It is important that you maintain a line of open communication with your banker: keep them informed of your progress and don't spring any surprises on them!

Incurring debt is scary and risky. To protect yourself, do not commit any personal funds set aside for the future to your business, such as retirement funds or kids' college funds. Also, avoid credit card debt at all costs—credit card interest rates are too high. Before you incur debt, try raising cash by selling anything of value that you no longer need or use—vacation homes, fallow land, jewelry, or cars. While you might want to think about borrowing from friends or family, be aware that failed ventures might sour your relationships.

As a last resort, you can consider borrowing from an angel investor. Angel investors are individuals with high assets and with experience or interest in your industry who are willing to help fund your start-up costs in exchange for some role within your business. While the money and advice they offer can be invaluable, you might be required to obtain their permission before making any serious business decisions. Essentially, you would be trading start-up funding for loss of personal control and perhaps some loss of profit. If you are interested in looking into this option, check out the Angel Capital Electronic Network (ACE-Net) at **activecapital.org/index.html**; it is sponsored by the SBA Office of Advocacy.

BUSINESS PLANS

If you plan to seek financial help from any source, the first thing you will be asked to do is to provide your business plan. Your franchiser may provide you with training materials, but writing a business plan for your individual franchise is your responsibility. A good business plan will give a clear picture of where you are and where you are headed, and – of course – how you plan to get there.

While business plans can be complicated and difficult to write, they are essential; you will find that as you write the plan, your ideas and plans will begin to take form and become clearer. A business plan is not only a tool with which to access financial assistance, it is also a means through which you can form a better idea of your own situation, goals, and progress. A good business plan will help you to think deeply and in detail about your business; to realistically assess your financial status and readiness; to understand your chosen market; and to obtain that needed funding from creditors and investors. Most importantly, it will help you to discover in which areas you can expect your franchiser to help you succeed and in which areas you will need to use your own devices. Do not write it, get your financing, and then file it away. Keep it out, read it often, revise it when necessary — use it to your advantage!

The following sections will provide you with an idea of how to write, organize, and present your business plan. Some useful resources are provided at the end of the chapter.

MAJOR ELEMENTS OF A BUSINESS PLAN

A good business plan comprises ten major elements. They are described below:

- **Executive summary.** This element describes the business as well as its opportunities and risks. It includes a summary overview of the target market, major competitors, financial outlooks, and your advantages and disadvantages over competitors. If you are seeking money with your plan, say this as well, and include comments on how you plan to put the money to use. If you are looking for a good management team, focus your summary on the kind of team members you wish to recruit and the benefits you will offer them. Alternatively, you could aim your plan at both of these groups at once.

This executive summary is the element of the business plan most widely read by those considering funding your business. If your executive summary is poor or even mediocre, prospective financiers will not even read the remainder of your plan. You want to draw the investor in during the first thirty seconds — any loss of interest in that time will cause the investor to pick up the next plan on his or her desk. You must make your executive summary succinct, yet thorough and engaging.

You can expect to devote anywhere from a paragraph to two pages to your executive summary. Be sure to put the most important and relevant information at the beginning. Remember, you need to draw the investor in within the first thirty seconds.

- **Mission statement.** This element will define who you are, the philosophies behind your operation, and the reason you are in business (or want to be). Your mission statement can address such issues as your philosophies toward the franchiser, your community, and employees, or any other factors you find relevant.

- **Business structure overview.** This element provides pertinent factual information such as your proposed start-up date, how and from whom the business was acquired, your equity and debt, and any accomplishments or setbacks.

- **Industry analysis and background.** This is the second most important element (after the executive summary). It contains graphical and numerical analyses of your industry, your competitors, and how you compare to them. You must discuss the size of your industry and its growth or decline; major competitors; market share among the competitors; customer base; factors that will contribute to the industry's success; forecasts (from respected sources) of your industry's future; and any legislative, environmental, or business trends that might influence the path of your industry.

- **Market analysis and strategy.** This element addresses your potential customer base, competition, location, and any market trends relevant to your business. You should also discuss your franchiser's expectations for your business. Use this part of the business plan to highlight your knowledge and understanding of your business.

- **Day-to-day operations description.** This element outlines your day-to-day operations, including employee positions, hiring strategies, payroll procedures, and customer service protocols.

- **Marketing plan.** This element will describe how you plan to promote and market your business. Include a description of your grand opening (which will often be coordinated with your franchiser) and any descriptions of systematic promotions. Also, be sure to describe how you will set prices and how you will offer promotional sales, if any.

- **Management and organizational structure.** This element will outline what positions need to be filled in your business, how many of these positions exist, and how you plan to fill them. You should also talk about wage and salaries and strategies for keeping your employees happy and productive. If you have already hired upper management, feel free to include biographies of them in this section. If you will be personally involved in running your business, include your own biography and plans for personal compensation.

- **Financing.** In this section, discuss your start-up costs and any future capital needs. This section should also contain a cash flow analysis and profit-and-loss forecasts for five or more years. Make sure this element is strong and supports all your analyses with plenty of facts and figures. You must show investors that you are serious about the long term and that you have the know-how and capital to make your business work.

- **Appendix.** Include any supporting material such as resumes, tax returns, and community or industry news articles.

Writing a business plan may sound like a daunting task, but it is absolutely necessary. Remember: this is only the first challenge of running your own business. If you are intimidated by or unwilling to write a business plan, then perhaps you should think twice before purchasing a franchise.

A BUSINESS PLAN TEMPLATE

While you can obtain business plan templates from the Internet or other sources, we provide a basic template in this section. We encourage you to examine different templates and find the one that works best for you and your business.

- **Cover sheet.** Include the name and location of your franchiser, your own name and contact information (address, voice number, cell number, fax number, e-mail address, and Web site), and the date the plan was written or revised.

- **The executive summary.** An example of an executive summary for a franchise that wants to convince a chain to accept it is shown below.

Jenkins Sports is a potential franchisee of Got Game Enterprises. Jenkins Sports is wholly owned by Sally Jenkins and is a Colorado corporation. Jenkins Sports operates two stores in Denver which will become part of the Got Game chain. Jenkins Sports has a 15-year history of operation at its current locations and enjoys strong sales and brand recognition. The plan is intended as a tool for integrating

Jenkins Sports into the Got Game family over the next three years. The company is self-financing the $125,000 in transition costs for becoming a Got Game franchise, broken out as follows: $75,000 for the franchising fee; $25,000 for new signage and advertising; and $25,000 for interior redesign and training. Jenkins Sports has an outstanding cash and credit position.

- **Table of contents.**

- **Section 1: The business.**

   — **Mission statement.**

   — **Business structure overview.** An example is provided below.

   Got Game Enterprises is a federally registered franchise founded in Los Angeles, California, in 1970. The company is currently registered in California, Utah, Nevada, Arizona, Idaho, and Colorado. There are five company-owned locations and 11 franchised locations in California, Idaho, and Arizona. The company was founded by Lawrence Thomas, who retired from managing daily operations in 1997. The company has been headed by CEO Jack Peterson since the retirement of Mr. Thomas. Franchisees of Got Game Enterprises generally are previously established local sporting goods stores with extensive experience in the sporting goods industry. Got Game Enterprises conducts screening of its franchisees, and each franchisee must be personally approved by Mr. Thomas. There is a short training program for new franchisees.

The franchise fee is $37,500 per store, which is high for a sporting goods franchise. A regional advertising fee of 1 percent of gross sales is charged to all franchisees, along with a 3 percent royalty on gross sales. The franchisees meet semi-annually, concurrent with the stockholders' meetings for Got Game Enterprises.

— **Industry analysis and background.**

— **Market analysis and strategy.** An example is provided below.

Jenkins Sports' first location is at 1729 Adelphia Boulevard, in the heart of the city's Fremont neighborhood. The store is the anchor of a strip mall containing 21 other stores, including a gymnasium, a health food store, and a sports medicine clinic. It receives good levels of traffic from health- and fitness-minded shoppers at the other stores in the center. Parking facilities are ample and well-lit, and the neighborhood is considered to be very safe. There is a significant level of traffic on the adjoining Lincoln Avenue, and there is congestion at both morning and afternoon rush hours. The store has approximately 8000 square feet and includes extensive office area, a training center, and an employee lounge. The delivery facilities have recently been modernized with new electric lift gates and three loading bays.

The primary customer bases for Jenkins Sports and Got Game Enterprises are similar: men (53 percent) and women (47 percent) between the ages of 13 and 65, with an average per-capita income of $32,500. According to a recent study by the Sports Council of America, 42 percent of adults in the Denver area have purchased or plan to purchase sporting goods equipment in the last year.

Analysis of the addresses provided by the current Jenkins Sports customers indicates that the median distance from the nearest store is 2.4 miles. Eighty-nine percent of all customers live within 3.7 miles of a Jenkins Sports store. Accordingly, we define our market area as the area within 4 miles of each Jenkins Sports store. Census data indicates that there are approximately 83,000 households within this area for the first store and 79,400 households within the area for the second store. This compares favorably with the Got Game Enterprises average of 67,500 households per store.

Advertising costs in the Denver area are within the average range for the country as a whole. However, ad costs overall may be somewhat higher because of Denver's large Hispanic population, many of whom speak only Spanish. It will be necessary to advertise both in English- and Spanish-language media.

There are a number of youth sports teams, intramural leagues, work-related teams, and other individual and group sports events and facilities in Denver. A substantial portion of Jenkins Sports marketing in the past has been outreach to these groups and teams, and this will continue to be a major component going forward.

There is a Gart Sports franchise store approximately 2.4 miles from the first Jenkins Sports store. This Gart Sports store is busy during the summer months but seems quiet at other times of the year. Prices at Gart stores are between 5 and 10 percent higher than at Jenkins Sports, and customer service is considerably slower. Gart Sports does no maintenance or repair work on equipment. Jenkins Sports maintains a strong repeat business customer base, with over 70 percent of our sales going to people who have shopped with us before. Our on-site maintenance and repair facility is cited by many customers as being a major factor in their decision to shop with us.

— **Day-to-day operations description.**

— **Marketing plan.**

— **Management and organization structure.** An example
is provided below.

*Sally Jenkins is the overall manager and executive officer
for Jenkins Sports. Sally has an MBA from Dartmouth and
more than 20 years of experience managing the two Jenkins
Sports outlets. Sally will be responsible for handling the
finances, marketing, and operations at both stores.*

*Richard Plowman is the director of marketing. Richard
has an MBA from the University of Colorado and was
previously a marketing analyst for Wilson.*

*Each store will have its own general manager who reports
directly to Sally after we become Got Game franchisees.
These management positions have not yet been filled, but we
have a number of outstanding candidates lined up.*

*Jenkins Sports uses stock clerks, cashiers, floor assistants,
and maintenance technicians. All employees are part-time
and do not receive health benefits. Jenkins Sports does*

provide one week of paid vacation for every 1,000 hours worked, and employees receive a 25 percent discount on merchandise.

Stock clerks are able to lift heavy objects, work without supervision, and keep track of inventory. Stock clerks must be able to use the computerized inventory system. We currently have a waiting list for stock clerks because the job has flexible hours and good pay ($11.50 per hour).

Cashiers interact directly with customers, handle money, and process returns. Cashiers must be able to use the computerized checkout system. There is a continual turnover of cashiers, with about 10 percent of our cashiers leaving in a given month, so we are continually hiring for the cashier positions. Cashiers are paid $9 per hour.

Floor assistants help customers find what they need and answer questions about the merchandise. Floor assistants are paid on a commission basis, receiving 10 percent of all sales they direct to the cashiers. Floor assistants must be knowledgeable about sports and sporting equipment and must be highly sociable and friendly. There is almost no turnover among our floor assistants, and we have no plans to hire more at this time.

Maintenance technicians work in the maintenance and repair shop. They perform warranty repairs and maintenance on a wide variety of sports equipment. Proficiency with tools, including laminators and gluing machines, is the primary qualification for this position. Maintenance technicians are paid $14.00 per hour and are difficult to hire; we are always recruiting new ones.

— **Financing.** A discussion of contracts and obligations is included below.

Jenkins Sports has signed a 10-year lease on its current locations, and there are eight years remaining on the lease. We are very satisfied with the current locations, and there is no plan to attempt to break the lease.

Jenkins Sports and Got Game Enterprises are expected to sign a franchise agreement in the next few weeks. This agreement will be for a period of twenty years, with renewal options. The franchiser will provide the rights to Got Game Enterprises' trade dress, a training process, and a set of operating manuals for the company's purchasing system. Got Game Enterprises will also provide technical support on its purchasing system and will provide advertising materials, cutouts, end caps, and stand ups at its discretion. Jenkins Sports does not have the right to go outside the Got

Games Enterprises purchasing system. Jenkins Sports will pay Got Game Enterprises a 1 percent advertising fee and a 3 percent royalty on all gross sales. Got Game Enterprises will allocate at least 75 percent of the advertising fee to buy ads within the Denver market. Jenkins Sports has the exclusive right to market sporting goods in the Denver market within a 50-mile radius of the city center.

Got Game Enterprises has termination rights but must pay a $50,000 termination penalty if it chooses to exercise its option. Jenkins Sports is free to sell its operations to a third party without the consent of Got Game Enterprises, but any purchaser must renegotiate all franchise agreements with Got Game Enterprises.

This contract is in line with the fair franchising standards of the American Association of Franchisees and Dealers (AAFD).

- **Section 2: Financial data.** This section should contain all pertinent financial documents, outlining the details of your financial operations. You can obtain such documents from your accountant or personal bookkeeper. Documents should include loan applications, a list of equipment, a list of supplies, balance sheets, a break-even analysis, profit and loss statements (a summary over three years and details by month for the first year and by quarters for the second and third years) along with any supporting assumptions, and a cash flow analysis.

BUSINESS PLAN RESOURCES

We recommend two publications that can help you devise and write your business plan. The first provides help for any business: published by Atlantic Publishing, you can purchase *How to Write a Great Business Plan for Your Small Business in 60 Minutes or Less* for $39.95 from **www.atlantic-pub.com**. It even comes with a free companion CD-ROM.

For those entering the food service industry we recommend Atlantic Publishing's *Opening a Restaurant or Other Food Business Starter Kit: How to Prepare a Restaurant Business Plan & Feasibility Study.* You can purchase this publication for $39.95 from **www.atlantic-pub.com**.

5 Getting Financing

This chapter will offer a brief review of the different sources of funding you may want to consider. Funding can be obtained in the public sector through government programs, or in the private sector through banks or private investors. As mentioned in the previous chapter, your franchiser might have a working partnership with a lender who will be willing to approve your loan request in a reduced amount of time. These loans are often more expensive than loans sought personally. We advise you to read this chapter thoroughly before accepting any loan offers made through your franchiser.

It's extremely important that you look around extensively for a loan. Comparison shopping quickly reveals that not all loans are created equal—some are more expensive or restrictive than others. When you factor in origination fees, account maintenance fees, and early payoff penalties, loan costs can differ greatly. Do not jump at the first offer. Begin examining your options early so that by the time you need the funding, you have compared several loan possibilities and have spoken to some potential investors. Your business plan will be your greatest asset during this process.

There are two ways to finance a loan. The first is with debt. This option includes loans, rent, leases, mortgages, and bonds. It involves a process whereby a borrower accepts money with the intent to pay the money back with interest. You become in debt to the lender. Usually, you need to secure your loan with some kind of capital. For example, a loan taken to purchase inventory might be secured by the inventory itself. If you default on the loan, the lender could legally seize your inventory. On the bright side, if you choose to finance with debt, you retain control over and ownership of your business.

Your other option is to finance with equity. In this arrangement you sell a portion of your ownership of the business to your lender in exchange for funds. The lender might stipulate certain terms. For example, he or she might want a part in running the business or a share of the earnings. Or he or she could opt to be a silent partner. While a partner can contribute much in the way of expertise and advice, you might find the interference to be more of a burden than a blessing. It depends on the experience and personality of the lender.

STEPS TO TAKE BEFORE APPLYING FOR A LOAN

Whether you finance with equity or debt, you will need to approach a lender in order to obtain funding. Be prepared. Lenders are looking for specific things, and if you are organized, up front, and ready to answer any questions, your chances of securing a loan increase greatly. You should prepare by addressing the four P's: (1) people, (2) purpose, (3) payment, and (4) protection.

People

How do you stand as a person? Are you trustworthy and reliable? Is your credit history strong? Do you have a solid history of repaying debts on time and in good form? If your credit record is spotty, don't wait for the lender to discover this on his own. Bring it to his attention. You do not want to appear as though you are hiding anything, and when addressed early, trouble spots often have a way of working themselves out.

Purpose

Be able to describe in detail the purpose of the loan and be ready to answer any questions about its use. Account for the loan in your business plan and make sure everything lines up. Address any potential risks and find a way to assure the lender that the risks far outweigh the gains.

Payment

Using your business plan, show that your cash flow will be strong enough to afford the loan repayments. Lenders want to know that you will be able to pay, and on time.

Protection

In the case that the business cannot make payments, show the lender what protections he has on his side. What secondary sources are available? Are they adequate to ensure the loan?

The amount of funding you need depends upon a number of factors, including the type of franchise you will be operating, its industry, the local market, and your personal financial state. By the time you approach a lender, you should already have a good idea of the amount you will need. This is the type of information you will have discovered while writing your business plan.

Do not expect too much information from the franchiser in terms of operational costs at the individual franchise level. The law does not require a franchiser to provide such figures. This is for the franchiser's own protection: if a franchisee falls short, he or she could sue the franchiser for having provided misleading information. In order to provide franchisees with some ability to estimate costs, franchisers will often provide the gross sales numbers of existing franchises. Such a disclosure allows the new franchisee to estimate costs and earnings while protecting the franchiser from making any unfulfilled promises.

START-UP COSTS

As discussed in the previous chapter, start-up costs are those costs you have before you begin business. They involve purchasing the franchise, setting up shop, purchasing initial inventory — basically, getting the ball rolling. Usually, start-up costs are financed through bank loans and personal assets.

OPERATING COSTS

In the beginning, do not expect to break even. Your operating costs will exceed your revenue for a time. You will need working capital to supplement your initial operating costs during this period. Usually, operating costs are funded by lines of credit, which are extended when you need them. While meeting monthly payments on lines of credit can be difficult, you can reduce your monthly debt expenditure by putting more money into the opening of the business and by lengthening the repayment period of the loan.

PERSONAL LIVING COSTS

Don't forget—while you are funding your business, you have to be sure that you are also making ends meet at home. You need to be sure that you are making enough to live. While many assume that business owners reap endless profits, this is not always the case, especially in the beginning. The most successful business owners pour revenue back into their business; before you start doing that make sure you are keeping enough for yourself. A good practice is to begin whittling down your living expenses before you start your new business, so you get used to living on a smaller amount of money. Be sure to save at least six months' earnings before purchasing your franchise.

APPLYING FOR THAT LOAN

Once you have your materials in hand and your mind wrapped around the problem, begin approaching lenders. Remember that you are applying for a business loan, not a personal loan, so you should be prepared to sell yourself. Expect 30-minute meetings with each lender. Bring along a neat, professional three-ring binder containing the following supportive documentation: (1) your expertly crafted business plan, (2) your franchise agreement, (3) revenue and expense projections (as discussed in the last chapter, these should be monthly for one year and quarterly for the next two years), (4) personal financial records, including your tax returns for the past three years, and (5) additional documents that might aid the lender in making a favorable decision. While individual lenders might require additional documents, these make up the minimum you should have in your proposal. Having a proposal that's professional and neatly presented will enable you to evaluate your own plan and position and will likewise impress the lender with your professionalism and ability to plan.

You can seek help from many different sources as you put together your loan proposal. For example, use whatever your franchiser can offer in the way of information and ideas. Also, contact your local SBDC for additional help (call (703) 448-6124).

It can take the lender anywhere from a few days to several months to review your proposal, so plan ahead. Be sure that you apply in time to receive the funds when you need them.

FEDERAL GOVERNMENT

The SBA administers many programs to help meet the needs of small business owners. These programs include guaranteed loans to small businesses that would otherwise have difficulty proving their ability to pay, including start-ups, businesses without collateral, or businesses that require an unusually long repayment period. In lieu of loan rejection, the lender would be guaranteed up to 80 percent by the SBA. While the SBA is willing to guarantee loans from many sources, not all sources are knowledgeable of and willing to work with the SBA, so do your research. Also, plan ahead — securing a loan through the SBA takes extra time.

The following are federal loan programs that the small business owners often take advantage of.

- 7(a) loans are part of an SBA loan program that guarantees loans up to $750,000. This program often requires the borrower to secure the loan with personal assets.

- LowDoc is a quickly processed guaranteed loan up to $100,000. Rather than using personal assets as security, this program features a one-page application focusing on the borrower's personal reputation and credit history.

- FASTRAC is another quickly processed guaranteed loan. This is the fastest loan; the credit check is performed by the lender and the loan approved under established SBA guidelines.

- Micro-loans are small loans of $250,000 or less offered by local governmental developmental agencies. These tend to have higher than average interest rates.

- 504 loans are also made through local economic development agencies, but the amount of financing available is tied to such indicators as job creation and asset assessment. The lending agency is limited to 40 percent of the total project but can lend no more than of $1 million.

STATE GOVERNMENT

While state financing programs vary, most are directed toward businesses that can improve the economic climate of the state through job creation and manufacturing. State funds are limited, but check with your local SBDC.

LOCAL GOVERNMENT

Local government financing options are usually limited to utility, facade, and landscaping enhancements. Local funding is frequently overlooked, so if you need these kinds of improvements, don't forget about this source.

COMMERCIAL AND PRIVATE SECTOR SOURCES

The first commercial lenders to come to mind are banks. Banks have special programs for business loans, as do savings and loan associations and credit unions. In particular, two lenders are known for specializing in franchise funding: the Center for Total Quality Franchising at (800) 733-9858 and Wells Fargo at (800) 359-3557.

Non-bank lenders also exist and should not be overlooked. Non-bank lenders are typically the most receptive to SBA-guaranteed loans and consist of for-profit private companies. They are located around the nation and are worth considering. Your franchiser might have an established relationship with such an organization, but while your loan will be approved more quickly, your costs may increase.

FRIENDS AND RELATIVES

For your initial down payment on a franchise, your own funds can often be combined with funds borrowed from friends and relatives. Before putting your personal relationships at risk, be sure your friends and relatives know the risks you are taking. Be sure also that they don't expect an immediate repayment—it could be months or years before you can afford to pay them back. If your business doesn't succeed, you may never be able to pay them back.

EQUITY INVESTORS

Getting the backing of equity investors may take extra effort. Most are more interested in dealing directly with franchisers than with individual franchisees. They want to deal with recognizable names and trademarks that possess strong franchise programs.

TABLE 5.1:
TELEPHONE DIRECTORY OF MISCELLANEOUS FINANCING SOURCES

SBA Answer Desk	800-827-5722
American Venture Capital Exchange	503-221-9981
National Association of Investment Companies	202-289-4336
National Association of Women Business Owners	312-322-0990
Small Business Investment Companies Directory (5BIC)	202-205-6510
Small Business Advancement National Center	501-450-5300

ONLINE DIRECTORY OF
MISCELLANEOUS FUNDING SOURCES

SBA Online	www.sba.gov/financing
Entrepreneurial Edge	www.edgeonline.com
Finance Hub	www.financehub.com
US AD ATA	www.usadata.com
Lending Rates	www.freeyellow.com
Venture Capital Marketplace	www.v-capital.com.au
Small Business Securities Issues	www.sec.gov
Area development (site and facility planning)	www.area-development.com

6 Conducting a Market Analysis

No matter the quality or value of your product, it will not sell if there is no demand. This is an important rule of thumb when selecting a franchise and it should never be overlooked. If you want to sell products, you need a customer base; before you attempt to sell your product in a particular market, you must be sure that the market supports the projected customer base for your product.

It's a common mistake to think that if you are investing in a franchise with multiple locations and proven success, you need not worry about market demand. Do not think that because the franchise has flourished in other areas, it will flourish in yours. You need to conduct, or have a professional conduct, extensive market research of your own particular area before investing in the franchise. You might hear stories of how some business owners simply open up shop and immediately begin succeeding. Those stories, if true, may be attributable simply to luck. Don't count on luck. Imagine the financial consequences of failing, and you will quickly realize that market research is an absolute must. Thorough market research will not only increase your chances of success, it will also give you an idea of how rapidly you can expect to expand, how much money you can expect to make, and other information important to the continued success of your business.

MARKET RESEARCH

Market research can be time-consuming and costly, but it is a necessary expense. A thorough and precise market research campaign will help you to answer many otherwise difficult questions and will give you an understanding of the trends, market, and customer base you can expect to encounter while operating your franchise. Specifically, you want to discover who your customers are and who future customers are most likely to be; you will also research where your customers typically live and their ages, ethnicities, and gender. You need to know how often they shop, why they shop, how they shop, why they choose one business over another, the products they prefer, and the products they dislike. Finally, understanding their media habits is crucial. Do they watch television, listen to the radio, browse the Internet, read the newspaper or use all of these media outlets?

Take good news with the bad. Do not cast off bad news; learn to work with it and deal with it, and if you can't, move on. Remember that some negative results might not be as bad as they first appear. If you find that your product does not have much of a market in your area, attempt to discover the reasons. Can you fix the problem? Will a fresh face with a new approach work, or is the problem more ingrained? Sometimes a particular franchise simply will not work in a given area. Take the time and spend the money to discover this fact before you purchase the franchise.

To conduct market research, you can choose from several approaches. The most expensive option is to hire an independent marketing research firm. You will benefit from their excellent research and statistical skills, but also pay a considerable fee. If you decide to go this route, make sure you select a company with experience in your market and industry.

A less expensive, although not cheap, option is to contact marketing professionals within the university setting. University business and marketing professors will often do private consulting. If you're lucky and can present your case as an interesting one, a professor might even incorporate your needed research into a class project, saving you money and providing you with the innumerable perspectives and quality research by students.

A third option is to conduct your own research. This is an especially attractive option if you have some knowledge of statistics and some research experience. Don't be afraid to learn what you need to know — you might want to consider taking a marketing class at your local college. You can also learn a lot simply by visiting the business and marketing section of your neighborhood bookstore.

If you decide to do your own research, you might begin by speaking with competitors. Although information gleaned from them should be taken with a grain of salt, if conditions are good, you can get some helpful insight. To avoid appearing threatening, think about approaching indirect rather than direct competitors. Also, think about not approaching them directly at all, but rather spending some time observing the activity at their places of business. To determine what customers are spending, watch what they purchase and use this information along with an approximation of how many customers you have seen enter the shop to determine the average spending level. Observe when customers do and do not shop, both daily and by seasons.

You will also need to gather data directly from customers. This can be done via survey or personal interview. You can also use observation — watch the customers of your competitors. Who are they? What did they buy?

In addition to the primary sources above, you will need to consult some secondary sources of information. Check research journals, magazines, government statistical publications, and other similar sources. Visit your local small business development center or speak directly to the appropriate local government officials. The latter will be particularly useful if you are looking for census data and projections (for example, is your area growing or shrinking, and who is moving in and out?). Finally, don't forget trade associations and your local chamber of commerce, both invaluable sources of useful information.

You might be able to gather important and relevant statistics and information from your franchiser; however, their information, while quality, might also be limited. Remember, they are not responsible for your individual success and research into your particular market is not their responsibility; therefore, they are unlikely to have any specifics that you can use. However, any more general information they can provide could be useful as a jumping-off point for your own research.

Don't forget about your fellow franchisees. Both current and retired franchisees working in the same business or industry can provide great information about sales, customers, and trends. While you probably won't get hard numbers and statistics from these sources, you can expect to receive more impressionistic advice and observations. Don't discount this kind of data. It can be just as useful and beneficial as numbers in a column.

CONDUCTING AN INDUSTRY ANALYSIS

Your franchise, like all businesses, will be part of a larger industry. Research into your industry as a whole will have to be conducted. Industries are not static; new technologies, changing demographics, and competitive industries will all influence the performance and success (or failure) of your business.

A thorough industry analysis will give you some insight into where your industry is currently thriving or suffering and may highlight areas or opportunities for improvement. It will also point you toward trends and technologies to which you should pay attention or in which you should invest. Any impending changes in technology or in the competitor landscape will have some effect on your business—will the changes be positive or negative? If the changes will be negative, why and how, and what, if anything, can you do to turn the negative into a positive? If you have the requisite knowledge and skills, you might be capable of creating a successful business within an ailing industry by providing the things the industry lacks. However, you might discover that the industry has deep problems that are impossible for you, or anyone, to solve. Obviously, discovering such facts before investing in your franchise is extremely important.

To conduct your industry analysis, begin by gathering information from the following five groups. First, speak to the people who would be your customers. You will not find a better source for determining what your industry should offer and whether or not it is offering it. Dissatisfied customers are a blessing if their complaints can be solved by creative restructuring; they are a curse if you realize that no amount of change can solve the problem and that the industry is inherently flawed.

Second, talk to your suppliers and distributors. They know standard practice and the business scenario of your competitors, and will also be up to date on trends and technology changes. They will be able to inform you accurately about demand and whether the industry is growing or shrinking.

Third, employees are a great source of information. While you want to filter out any biased information gleaned from employees, they will be able to tell you, from direct experience, how the industry is faring. They are a particularly good source of information about more local market trends, but don't look to employees for the bigger picture.

Fourth, don't overlook your competitors. From this source, you will be able to get an idea of whether the industry is competitive or whether your competitors create new customers for you and others. In other words, is the industry competitive or cooperative? A simple examination of marketing strategies among your competitors can probably give you a good idea of this.

Finally, once again, consult with other franchisees, both past and present. Especially if they are successful, they will be able to give you an accurate picture of the industry as a whole.

In addition to the above five groups, you might want to think about talking to journalists and other analysts who specialize in your industry. The objectivity of their information will be valuable, and they will be able to reflect upon the bigger picture. Legal and financial professionals with a large number of clients in the industry might also be able to provide you with a different picture.

Whatever you do, don't go into your industry analysis without educating yourself. By knowing the basics of your industry — its customer base, its products, its major players, and any technological, legal, or environmental influences — you will be armed with the knowledge needed to ask the right questions and to temper any information with accurate personal assessments. You must be able to understand the information you are given and have the ability to place it in its appropriate position within the industry as a whole.

Also, consider the wide array of secondary sources available to you. Again, trade magazines, research journals, newspapers, and government publications will provide you with valuable insight. Whatever sources you use, be sure to answer the key questions:

how large is my industry? What is its potential for growth? What is its geographic, economic, legal, and cultural environment? What trends or patterns are there? What is its profit potential? Who are my major competitors, and who are the industry leaders? Who composes the customer base and how do they think? Who are the major suppliers and how are products delivered to the customer? What are some of the technological issues affecting my industry?

CONDUCTING A MARKET ANALYSIS

Once you have done some preliminary investigation into your market and have conducted an industry analysis, you will need to determine whether your business is appropriate for your market. Most importantly, you need to ascertain whether there are enough customers in your market to support the success of your business.

You can often obtain a profile of your typical potential customer from your franchiser. It is smart to work with the demographic information they provide, but if you have a plan to expand to other demographics, more power to you. Basically, you should examine your collected data, compare it to the model demographics supplied by your franchiser, and determine if there are enough customers in your area to make your business flourish. If your primary target customer is a 30-year-old, college-educated, stay-at-home mom, you do not want to start your business in a market composed mostly of single males. If you can't make the numbers work, consider investing in a franchise that will work in your area. There are plenty from which to choose.

If the numbers do work out in your favor, your next step will be finding a location for your business that takes advantage of what the market  has to offer. Research the traffic patterns of your target customers. Discover housing densities and recreational areas popular with your target customers. Find out where they live, where they work, where they eat, where they party, and where they shop, and set up your business right in the thick of things. In particular, think about the following characteristics of sites under your consideration: What is the neighborhood population and demographic distribution? What is the typical income around the location? How rampant is crime? Are people moving into or out of the area surrounding the location? What developments might affect the location in the future? Most importantly, how many of your target customers live within walking and driving distance of the location? How many live within a five-mile radius?

In conducting your research, you will more than likely discover some unexpected problems with your business plan. You might find that your customer base is smaller than anticipated or that some impending technological advancement will affect your business in a way you hadn't expected. Remember, you cannot ignore such problems. Rather, realize that had you not discovered the issues in advance, the impact on your business could have been devastating. Use your new-found knowledge to solve the problem and redirect your business plan. Then, you will be able to approach any potential investors with a thorough market analysis accompanied by a sound business plan.

Creating Financial Statements

C reating financial statements is an important step toward making an informed decision about your franchise purchase. And, after the purchase, you'll have a useful tool in helping you stay on track financially.

PROJECTED INCOME STATEMENTS

A projected income statement is an invaluable tool. It will help you estimate your approximate income and expenses in the short term, from months to a few years. The more time your estimate covers, the less accurate it will be, although sometimes, longer-term estimates are necessary. Whatever its accuracy, a projected income statement will give you a gauge to judge your financial progress.

If you find that your projected income statement is highly inaccurate over the course of months, for example, if it is off by 20 percent or more, rewrite your statement, taking into account new information gleaned from your operations. While you can expect some variation from your projections over the very short term, you will find that over time your projections and actual earnings and expenses will even out in most cases.

Projecting your income is important because it will rarely vary substantially. You might experience seasonal highs and lows, but on a year-to-year basis, you can expect comparable incomes. In calculating your estimated expenses, you need to be as thorough as possible, while at the same time realizing that some expenses will be variable from month to month (others will be fixed). In addition, some expenses will take you by surprise. Whatever numbers you use, make sure to mark them with footnotes explaining how you arrived at each figure.

To account for unexpected expenses, be as conservative as possible in your estimates. Exaggerate your expenses and understate your income, but don't be so conservative that you undercut yourself on funds available for working capital.

Projected income statements are usually standardized, so that you can systematically compare your projected income statement with past income statements and with income statements from other businesses and franchises. A suggested format, shown in Figure 7.1, is based on the standard used by the Uniform System of Accounts for Restaurants.

FIGURE 7.1:

A SAMPLE INCOME STATEMENT FORMAT

SALES	
Food Sales	XX.XX
Beverage Sales	XX.XX
Total Sales	**$XX.XX**
COST OF SALES	
Food	XX.XX
Beverage	XX.XX
Total Cost of Sales	**$XX.XX**
Gross Profit = Total sales – Total Cost of sales	
Other Income	XX.XX
Total Income = GP + Other Income	
CONTROLLABLE EXPENSES	
Payroll	XX.XX
Employee Benefits	XX.XX
Direct Operating Expenses	XX.XX
Advertising and Promotion	XX.XX
Utilities	XX.XX
Administration and General	XX.XX
Maintenance	XX.XX
Total Controllable Expenses	XX.XX
Income before Occupancy Costs = **Total Income – Total Controllable Expenses**	
OCCUPANCY COSTS	
Rent	XX.XX
Property Taxes	XX.XX
Other Taxes	XX.XX
Property Insurance	XX.XX
Total Occupancy Costs	XX.XX
Income before Interest and Depreciation = **Income before Occupancy – Occupancy Expense**	
Interest	XX.XX
Depreciation	XX.XX
Restaurant Profit	XX.XX

Other Deductions	XX.XX
Income Before Taxes	XX.XX
Taxes	XX.XX
Total Interest and Depreciation	**XX.XX**
Net Profit (Loss) = Income before interest and depreciation – Interest and Depreciation w/ double underline	

ESTIMATING INCOME AND CASH FLOW

In order to secure funding from financial institutions, it is often necessary to create accurate three-year income and cash flow projections. Income and cash flow projections should adhere to the following format:

- A summary over three years;

- Projections for the first year by month (this can be extended for businesses that do not break even after the first year);

- Projections for the second and third years by quarter (each quarter is three months).

If you are considering taking over an existing franchise, ask to see the income and cash flow projections of the franchise for the past two years. If necessary, check tax returns to substantiate any claims.

SALES FORECASTS

Predicting your sales is not a simple task, especially if you are just starting out. Every business and industry experiences seasonal and yearly variations in sales. If you are not sure where to begin, try the following technique: create a table with three columns, one labeled "low," one labeled "high," and in the middle, one labeled "most likely." In the "low" column, enter what you expect your sales to be in the worst possible case. In the "high" column, enter your dream sales figures. In the "most likely," enter a value between the low and the high. This column will probably contain the most accurate sales estimates. The same method can be used to forecast your expected expenses.

To check your predictions, find published sales and expense figures in your trade or industry. These figures come from existing businesses and can provide a good point of comparison, but remember that figures may vary regionally.

FIGURE 7.2:

SALES FORECAST FOR (MONTH, YEAR) TO (MONTH, YEAR)

Sales:	Low	Most Likely	High
Draft beer			
Bottled beer			
Liquor			
Wine			
Nonalcoholic beverages			
Food			
Total Sales:			

STARTING THE INVESTIGATION

Creating a projected income statement before purchasing your franchise might be a helpful exercise. It will tell you in no uncertain terms whether the franchise will match your financial needs. To begin to put one together, first contact the franchiser of the business in which you are interested. For example, you could consult *Bond's Franchise Guide*, a guide covering more than 2000 franchises that has detailed profiles of franchisers. You can also look at the franchise listing in the back of this book. When you find a franchise that seems like a good fit, contact the organization's development department. Your contact will most likely result in your reception of an informational packet and a UFOC.

QUIZZING THE CURRENT FRANCHISES

Once you have reviewed the UFOC, if you are still interested in investing in the franchise, begin speaking one-on-one with the franchiser's representatives and other franchisees. For starters, turn to the section of the UFOC that lists contact information for current franchises. If this is not included in your UFOC, ask for it; the franchiser will furnish it separately.

Call as many franchisees as possible, including voluntary or involuntary retirees from the business, and be sure to include a sizable cross section of businesses in order to get the most reliable results. Ask all the important financial questions, inquire about profits and losses, earnings and expenses, and so on.

CALCULATING POTENTIAL SALES, CASH FLOW, AND PROFIT

Your next step is to begin calculations. This is a necessary step as it will help you to determine if the franchise will be profitable. It is not always simple, but don't let that discourage you. Skipping this step could be financial suicide.

While the FTC does not require franchisers to provide sales and figures of past franchises or sales estimates to prospective franchisees, some franchisers may include an "earnings claim" in their UFOC. Because franchisers are hesitant to make any estimates, this claim typically takes the form of past sales figures from existing franchisers. Franchisers fear that should a franchisee not reach that level of sales, the franchiser could be sued for misrepresentation. As of now, about 32 percent of franchisers provide an earnings claim in their UFOC; this percentage will probably increase under competitive pressure from other franchisers. If you do find an earnings claim in your franchiser's UFOC, it will probably look something like Figure 7.3.

FIGURE 7.3:
SAMPLE FRANCHISING EARNINGS CLAIM
(BURGER KING AND HOLIDAY INN)

Burger King Corporation, franchiser of Burger King fast-food restaurants, supplies Average Unit Sales estimates in Item 19 of the 1996 UFOC. Restaurants used in calculation of Average Sales consisted of 5901 "traditional" and 495 "nontraditional." Nontraditional sites include: (1) "expressway" facilities serving a limited menu; (2) restaurants at institutional locations (such as airports, colleges, hospitals, tourist locations); (3) co-branded facilities and (4) restaurants at double drive-thru facilities.

Median Sales for franchised traditional restaurants is $1,081,970 and $716,341 for nontraditional restaurants.

RESTAURANT MEDIAN SALES

Traditional Restaurants	Company	Franchise
Low Annual Sales	$309,073	$203,478
High Annual Sales	$2,368,460	$2,640,276

Median Sales	$1,109,095	$1,081,970
Nontraditional Restaurants	**Company**	**Franchise**
Low Annual Sales	$302,545	$66,740
High Annual Sales	$2,199,993	$3,796,189
Median Sales	$547,311	$716,341

Item 19 of the Uniform Franchise Offering Circular of December 31,1996. Burger King Corporation, 1777 Old Cutler Rd., Miami, FL 33157.

Holiday Hospitality Franchising, franchiser of the Holiday Inn Hotels, offers information on the Average Room Rate, Average Occupancy Rate and Average Revenue Per Available Room in Item 19 of the UFOC. The following information is for the fiscal year October 1996 to September 1997. The averages that follow represent information for all 1884 franchised Holiday Inn hotels in operation.

Average Room Rate	$68.18
Average Occupancy Rate	65.6%
Average Revenue Per Available Room (RPAR)	$44.74

Average Room Rate was calculated by dividing total amount of room rental revenues by total number of guest rooms rented. A total of 584 hotels, or 31 percent, in the study achieved or surpassed this average room rate.

Average Occupancy Rate was calculated by dividing the number of guest room nights reported rented by total number of rooms available for rent. A total of 868 hotels, or 46.1 percent in the study achieved or surpassed this rate.

The RPAR was calculated by multiplying the Average Room Rate for each hotel by its Average Occupancy Rate. A total of 661 hotels, or 35.1 percent, in the study achieved or surpassed this RPAR.

In Item 19 of its UFOC, Jiffy Lube International, Inc., franchiser of Jiffy Lube "quick lube" service centers, discloses earnings claims. There were 413 stations that were in operation for the full 12 months of 1996—all were company-owned. The following table divides the 413 stations into three groups on the basis of median gross sales level.

CENTERS BASED ON MEDIAN GROSS SALES LEVELS

Number of Centers	Range of Gross Sales	Median Gross Sales
138 Centers	$181,032 - $417,490	$350,374
138 Centers	$417,555 - $566,127	$475,283
137 Centers	$567,120 - $1,337,743	$738,931

CALCULATING AVERAGE GROSS SALES

Without the benefit of an earnings claim you might find it necessary to create your own average gross sales estimate. To calculate a franchise program's average gross sales, you can take the following steps:

- First, check public records to determine the total amount of royalty payments made to the franchiser by individual franchisees;

- Second, check the UFOC for the standard royalty rate (the percentage rate paid by franchisees to the franchiser);

- Third, count the number of full-time franchises in operation, excluding company-owned establishments;

- Next, divide the total royalty figure by the number of operating franchises;

- Finally, divide the number obtained in step four by the royalty rate. You will end up with an estimated gross sales figure per franchise.

Table 7.1 provides a table format useful in calculating average gross sales.

TABLE 7.1:
WORKSHEET FOR AVERAGE GROSS SALES PER FRANCHISE

1.	Total Royalty Amount franchiser receives from franchisees:	$XXXX.XX
2.	Royalty Rate	$XXXX.XX
3.	Number of Operating Franchised Units (no company-owned units)	$XXXX.XX
4.	Average Royalty Payment per franchisee (Total Royalty Amount [# 1] divided by Number of Franchised Units)	$XXXX.XX
5.	Average Gross Sales per franchisee (Average Royalty Payment per franchisee divided by the Royalty Rate)	$XXXX.XX

PROJECTING CASH FLOW

Your business's cash flow is the difference between expenditures and income; this figure can serve as a way to determine your estimated cash needs. This is also called a cash flow analysis. By knowing when you will experience an excess or shortage of cash, you will be able to decide if you have enough working capital to see your business through.

As an example, if the initial layout for your franchise — including purchase cost, fees, equipment, and rent — is $50,000, and you have $70,000 to fund your business, you will be left with $20,000 working capital. You can use a cash flow analysis to determine whether your $20,000 is enough to operate your business prior to making a profit. After you calculate your projected annual sales figure, you will need to consider the following.

- For a cash business (no credit transactions), you will draw in money equal to your sales. However, for a business in which you allow credit transactions, you may not receive payments for one or two months, depending upon your credit terms. You will need to work this into your cash flow analysis. It is advisable to assume a month extra before payment before you account for late payments.

- A list of expenditures needs to be created per month. Expenditures can include overhead costs such as utilities, rent, loan repayments, advertising, cost of goods, payroll, insurance, and royalty payments. The last should be divided according to expenditures with fixed costs and expenditures with variable costs.

Once you have computed these figures, add your estimated sales to obtain a figure for your total available cash. Then add expected expenditures and subtract your expenditures from your cash intake. This will help you obtain your total available cash. If you plan to pay yourself a salary or if you have a loan, you will need to subtract your salary and/or loan amortization amount for a final available cash figure. Amortization is similar to depreciation, but on a nontangible item. Just as you would depreciate a piece of equipment over years, your franchise will also depreciate. If you bought your franchise for $25,000 it might amortize (or depreciate) $4,000 per year. This should be included in your total expenditures.

Compare this final available cash figure to your working capital. If your available cash is negative for several months and you cannot cover your losses with your working capital, then you might need to consider investing in a more affordable franchise. However, if your working capital is sufficient, then the franchise is a good option for you.

PROFIT AND LOSS STATEMENT

The final financial statement that needs to be prepared is a profit and loss statement (P&L). This should cover a two-year period. If you have already calculated your annual sales and completed your cash flow analysis, then creating a P&L should be short work.

- From the sales estimate for your first year, subtract the cost of sales or of goods sold (cost of goods = beginning inventory + purchases – ending inventory). The resulting figure is your gross margin number.

- Take the total expenditures from your cash flow analysis and subtract it from your gross margin number. This is your net income (your income before taxes; if the number is negative, you have a loss).

If you need to create a P&L for subsequent years, try to estimate a reasonable percentage increase of both sales and cost of sales for those years. You can use the advice of fellow franchisees to estimate this percentage. Subtract these two figures to arrive at an estimated net income for these years. In most cases, you will experience a larger net income as years go by.

FINAL WORDS

Creating these financial documents and accounts may be tricky, confusing, and time-consuming, but their creation is a necessary step. By creating these tools, you will be better able to determine whether a particular franchise will meet your needs in terms of profitability and cost. Also, you will be able to decide if the franchise is financially sound in its own right.

Do not be afraid to enlist the aid of a financial professional, such as an accountant, in creating these statements. You do not want to take any shortcuts; if you are not personally cut out for this kind of work, spend the money to hire someone who is. These statements are that important.

CHAPTER 8

Locating Your Franchise

FINDING THE BEST LOCATION FOR YOUR FRANCHISE

One of the most important decisions you will make after you purchase your franchise is choosing its location. The success and profitability of your business will be directly related to the appropriateness of the location you choose. While some factors might seem important at the outset, such as its proximity to you or its cost, the most important aspect of the location is its relation to your target customer base.

If you will be operating an off-site business, you might be able to use your own home as a base of operations. In this case, traffic patterns and visibility will not play a large role in the success of your franchise; space requirements might be most important. In contrast, if you will be running an on-site business, visibility and beneficial traffic patterns will rise to the top of your list of priorities.

The market research you conducted before purchasing your franchise will come into considerable play when you begin looking for an ideal location. Use demographic information to determine if a particular location will provide the right customer base for your business. In addition, think about how your products or services fit into a customer's daily life and try to locate your business along a suitable path or around complementary businesses.

Can you expect help from the franchiser in selecting a location? In some cases, a franchiser won't help you find the right location, but will have to approve of and accept your choice. In other cases, a franchiser might provide some help or even insist on finding the location itself.

HOW TO EVALUATE YOUR LOCATION

Determine what factors are most important to the success of your business. Will visibility matter? What about parking capacity? Some features of a site will be more expensive than others, but don't skimp on the things necessary for success. The following factors are very important:

- What is the flow of traffic around your location? Is the location easily accessible from all directions? What changes in traffic lights or patterns are planned that might alter the flow around your location, and how will those changes affect your business?

- Will you require visibility? If so, is the location suitable? Can potential customers see it easily?

- What are your planned business hours, and what are the hours of surrounding businesses? If you plan to have late hours, do not choose a location with surrounding businesses that close in the evening as your customer traffic could be compromised.

- Does the location have enough parking space, or room to add more if needed? If you need to add more, how much is it going to cost?

- If you will be running an urban business, is your location easy to access for users of public transportation?

- What changes is the surrounding neighborhood experiencing? Is it thriving and growing or is it declining?

- Will your location be able to provide the space you need?

- What competitors are in the location's vicinity, and will they negatively or positively affect your business?

FINANCIAL CONSIDERATIONS

In most cases you will find yourself leasing from a landlord directly, and sometimes the franchiser will act as a guarantor on your behalf. In other cases the franchiser might take out the lease and sublet to you. If you find yourself in this position, be sure that there is a clause in the lease stating that if the franchiser defaults, you have the right to take over the lease and make up for any late payments.

You might purchase a franchise that requires you to buy a location rather than lease. If this is the case, expect a higher initial cost as well as a larger commitment to staying in that location. If you will need to purchase land on which to build a new store, be sure that you receive building cost estimates before signing a purchase agreement for the land.

CONSTRUCTING A LOCATION

Unless your landlord agrees to "build to suit," you will be responsible for building your own location. The following subsections outline the steps you will need to take to do this successfully.

Step 1: Hire a contractor. Ask around to be sure you hire a contractor with a good reputation for service and cost. Ensure that your contractor will provide a completion bond that guarantees compensation to you if construction on your location is delayed, causing you financial loss. Most importantly, do not allow work to start until you and your contractor have signed a legally binding contract specifying the work to be done and any legal conditions. For example, specify that your contractor waives the right to a mechanic's lien on your location in the case of a faulty or late payment; your landlord may require such a waiver anyway. If your plans include a large building, be sure that you specify in the contract your right to withhold payment in the case of delayed progress of the construction as determined by the architect. Also, do not make full payment until the work is completed; holding back 10 percent of the total cost until completion is more than reasonable.

Step 2: Know your signage requirements. Before signing your lease, be sure that any signage you plan to erect is approved by your landlord. Get his or her approval in writing. You might also need to get approval for your signage from local authorities, so be sure that your lease specifies an effective date contingent upon all necessary signage approval.

Step 3: Acquire licenses and permits. If you will require licenses and permits (and you undoubtedly will), your agreement should indicate the responsible party. In addition, you should ensure that your franchise will not violate any zoning ordinances or your landlord's certificate of occupancy. Finally, be certain that your contractor displays building permits in full compliance with the law; you might be required to obtain these permits on behalf of the contractor. Use the guidance of an attorney in all these matters.

NEGOTIATING A LEASE

Negotiating a lease is not a simple process, and there can be many hidden fees and clauses which can affect your business negatively. We cannot provide you with any standards to follow, but remember that the best possible lease will cater to the needs of both you and your landlord. Most importantly, do not sign any lease without the review and approval of a legal representative. Leases are legally binding contracts and are not to be taken lightly.

Keep in mind the four things you need to do before signing any lease: (1) be prepared with knowledge of possible clauses and their meanings; (2) review the lease with your attorney and have him or her present during any negotiations or signing; (3) keep an open mind about your location, and **do not accept lousy terms just because you think a location is "perfect"**; (4) be patient and take your time.

THINGS TO CONSIDER WHEN LEASING WITHIN A SHOPPING CENTER

If your location is within a shopping center, there are a few things you should keep in mind. First, you want to look for an anchor store, which is a large store known to draw significant numbers of customers. This store will most likely increase your customer flow. If there is an anchor store about to open in your shopping center, you should negotiate lower rent payments for the months before it opens. Likewise, if the anchor store closes, your rent should be reduced. However, you should not pay higher rent if additional anchor stores open.

Sometimes tenants of a shopping center form a merchants'

association, and your lease might require that you join this association. Joining an association will have effects on your advertising budget and plans, so learn all the implications of membership before signing. In addition, you should get to know all the costs associated with common area maintenance in your complex. At times, these costs could be higher than your rent. Your best bet is to make sure that your contributions are capped according to your gross revenue and that all administrative fees are also capped. In addition, if your contribution is based upon your square footage, it should be determined as a percentage of all square footage in the complex that can be leased.

Finally, do not allow any agreement stating that your landlord can move your location within the shopping center at will. This can significantly hurt your business.

THINGS TO CONSIDER WHEN SUBLETTING FROM YOUR FRANCHISER

If you sublet from your franchiser, obtain a written agreement from the landlord and attempt to have any administrative fee charged by your franchiser waived. In addition, you should be provided copies of all notices and communications sent and received between the franchiser and the landlord. These can come either directly from the landlord or from the franchiser. This way, should any problems be apparent or should any discounts be granted, you will also benefit.

If your franchiser serves as the tenant of your location, you will probably legally sublet from them. In this case, you should know that your franchiser may form a corporation as the tenant in order to shield the parent company from legal and financial liability in the case of a suit. If you ever need to sue your franchiser in its tenant capacity, do not expect much in the way of compensation.

CHAPTER

9 Marketing Your Franchise

While the impressions your customers receive when purchasing your product or service are crucial to success, just as important is your ability to get them into your store in the first place. This is what marketing is all about. You want to attract them, sell to them, and get them to come back for further purchases. An effective marketing plan will accomplish this.

A marketing plan can be broken down into four essential elements: (1) product, (2) price, (3) promotion, and (4) place. Some marketing texts refer to these as the "Four Ps." First, you need to have a sufficient supply of the products that customers want and need. Second, your products should be priced so that customers feel they are getting value for their money, particularly when compared to other options. Third, you need to think about how you are going to present your products and get customers to want them enough to buy. Finally, how will your products be delivered?

FINDING YOUR CUSTOMERS

Your first task to is get customers to your front door. To do so, they need to know you exist and how to find you. Using the resources available, you must construct a marketing plan that will allow customers to find you and that will convince them of their need for you.

Branding is an essential step toward this goal. Branding refers to the image you create in the minds of your customers when they think about your business. Through branding, you can construct the reality you desire — a personality for your business, products, or services. This personality should reflect upon the customers in a way that will make them feel better about themselves by using your product. While branding is effective, it is also time-consuming and costly and typically requires the aid of a public relations or advertising firm.

If you don't have the funds to develop branding, you could always rely on word of mouth. You would be surprised how quickly a good reputation spreads. Simply by asking all your friends and family to mention your business to acquaintances you can build a reputation and solid customer base more quickly than you ever thought possible. Most importantly, this strategy costs next to nothing to implement.

Whether you go for an expensive branding campaign, an inexpensive word of mouth campaign, or something in between, there are certain steps you should take before initiating any marketing strategies.

- **You should have a thorough understanding of your business,** your products or services, and your goals. This includes having an understanding of the customers you are trying to attract.

- **You will not sell products if customers do not have a need for those products.** When marketing, do not sell your product, but rather, sell a solution to customer needs.

- **Get the right message.** A handy and unique slogan is a great marketing tool; your customers will remember you and what you stand for if your slogan is good. Sometimes, your franchiser will provide a standard slogan.

- **Use the right media to reach your customers.** Advertise in the papers and magazines your customers read, and use the right blend of television and radio. Any research you conduct in this area will be well worth the time and money. And remember, customers need to hear your ad numerous times for it to be effective, so find the right media outlet and use it again and again.

- If possible, **use celebrities** to market your products or services.

- **Gauge the effects of your efforts and continue to use any winning strategies.** Discard ads or slogans that don't seem to be effective.

EFFECTIVE ADVERTISING

If you are part of a larger franchise network, you will be best served by forming partnerships with fellow franchisees around the country. If you pool your advertising assets, large national campaigns can be launched that will help you. If you run a smaller franchise, most of your advertising will probably remain at the local level. For larger franchises, expect to spend up to 60 percent of your advertising dollars on national campaigns. For smaller franchise owners, tailor your advertising to your expenses — begin with the cheapest form, measure your results, and go from there.

Radio Advertising

Contact local radio stations and inquire about their target demographic (most stations will cater to a specific group of people). If their demographic matches your target demographic, inquire about advertising costs. You will find that they are surprisingly affordable.

Telephone Advertising

Telemarketing is an option, but one that should be used carefully, if at all. Most people dislike telemarketing calls, and a recent slew of laws barring marketing calls can make it a difficult strategy. If you do use telemarketing, limit your hours to noninvasive ones (for instance, don't call during dinner hours) and make sure to use other advertising strategies as well.

Sponsor

Become a sponsor of a children's community sports team or local events (such as fairs or clubs). This will give you exposure while also emphasizing your interest in being a part of the community. Another option is to sponsor awards for academic or athletic achievements or give to charity in the name of your business.

Advertise in Print Media

Careful placement of a professionally designed advertisement in print media is a must. Some options include targeted newspapers, newsletters, or the phone book.

Direct Mail

While costs can be high and the rate of return isn't astounding, direct mail can earn you new customers and will get your name out there. To cut down on postage costs, try handing out flyers. Including a coupon in your mailings is one way to increase your customer base.

SOME NOTES ON CUSTOMER SERVICE

While marketing will get you customers, only good customer service will keep them coming back. Customer service and marketing go hand-in-hand. When you launch a marketing campaign, you try to meet certain customer needs to attract them. Once you have attracted them, you must actually meet these needs to keep them coming back. Any amount of good marketing will do you no good if you cannot offer and maintain exemplary customer service.

One way to gauge your success is to simply ask your customers how you are performing and whether you are meeting their needs satisfactorily. You already know your target demographic, and you have marketed to them, but once you get customers in your store, you should begin to meet their needs as individuals rather than as a group. Getting feedback is as simple as requesting that customers fill out a questionnaire or instituting an anonymous feedback card system. For more in-depth feedback, try starting a callback system (with your customers' permission, of course).

You should ask your customers about such things as pricing, inventory, cleanliness, professionalism, and other aspects of your business that might affect whether or not they return to do business with you. Remember that word of mouth is a powerful thing that can work for you or against you: your customers could just as easily tell their friends about the rudeness of your cashiers as they could about their professionalism. Keep a check on customer impressions by getting feedback.

Always demonstrate honesty and integrity. Try to solve all customer complaints, but do not compromise your own professionalism to do so. If you treat your customers fairly and with respect, you will usually get the same treatment in return. If a customer leaves having had a problem solved professionally, he or she is more likely to give you another chance to get it right. Remember, however, that a customer's experience will stick with him or her a long time. It may be years, if ever, that a customer who left dissatisfied will give your business another go, especially with so many other businesses that might be able to fill his or her needs.

Never forget: your customers are your most important asset.

10 Managing Employees

U nless you have a very small business, you will need to concentrate most of your time on managing your business. Daily operations should be left to employees. Hiring them can be a daunting task if you are new to the job. Don't put off hiring employees until the last minute, and don't go into the task unprepared. This chapter will give you some pointers to enable to you hire the right employees at the right time.

Your first step you should be to consult the information provided by your franchiser addressing the time it will take for you to find, hire, and train employees. If your training time will be approximately one week, and you need five workers to start, plan on hiring five workers one week before opening. Do not hire your workers too late in an attempt to save money, as your business will ultimately suffer. If you are not sure how much time your workers will need for training or if you don't know how many starting employees to hire, remember that your fellow franchisees can be a great source of information.

When hiring staff, you need to know three things: (1) where to look for employees, (2) how to interview the candidates and assess their skills, depending upon the position for which they are interviewing, and (3) how to manage your employees once they have been hired and begin working.

WHERE TO FIND NEW HIRES

Depending on the job market, you may have trouble finding suitable employees, or you may be overwhelmed with applications. Either way, locating a qualified employee pool is easy if you use the resources available to you.

- Posting "help wanted" signs can attract applicants, especially if you are building a new location; the construction will have already generated some notice.

- Use the placement programs offered by the government to advertise your need for employees to those currently unemployed.

- Contact local temp agencies; you can often hire temps on a permanent basis, although the agency may charge a fee.

- If you are located near a college or university, or even a high school, advertising for needed help on or around campus will win you a certain pool of part-time laborers. The job fairs hosted by such institutions are also a good starting point.

- Churches and other nonprofit organizations will often host job referral programs for the needy or the unemployed.

- Senior citizens are becoming increasingly involved in the work force as part-time employees; try advertising around retirement homes and other places where seniors congregate.

- Once you are established, do not forget that your current employees will recommend friends to hire if they are satisfied with their working environment.

WHAT TO LOOK FOR

One big mistake you should try to avoid is hiring based upon technical skills and experience alone. While technical skills are important for many positions, it is often possible to teach skills through training. But many of the "person" characteristics that make a good employee can't be taught. For example, it is possible to train just about anyone to use a pizza oven, but for employees in customer service people, you want that extra spark, that knack

with people that can't be taught. In other words, you should think about the personal traits that a position requires in addition to the skills necessary to work that position. Measure experience against personality and skills against education, and come up with a description of the perfect employee for each position. When interviewing, use that description as your model for hiring the right person for the job.

Another mistake to avoid is an inaccurate description of the position. If you have found the right employee, you should be sure that the employee understands the position fully. Any surprises or faulty expectations can turn the perfect employee into a disgruntled mess if he thinks he was misled. When crafting your job descriptions, include information on any skills or abilities required; the difficulty or complexity of any tasks required; the repetition and variety expected; the amount of responsibility that will be afforded in terms of supervision and decision-making; any communication skills needed; the amount of interaction expected between the employee and other employees and between the employee and customers; and your expectations of accuracy and precision. Also discuss the hours the employee is expected to work (and if this is static or changes from week to week), your vacation and benefits package, if any, and accumulation of overtime, if offered.

By writing precise job descriptions you will not only attract truly interested applicants, but you will be able to fit the best employee into each position. This will take the guesswork out of choosing the right employee.

INTERVIEWING AND HIRING

Organize your interview procedures and questions ahead of time: be prepared. You should ask pertinent questions, but you should also be sure to vary the questions in terms of response type. For example, make sure there is a mix of "yes-or-no" and open-ended questions. Remember that most people will not answer a yes-or-no question in a way that will make them appear unsuitable, so try to ask questions that may help you to eliminate applicants in an open-ended way. For example, rather than asking "Are you punctual?" ask "Describe your punctuality habits."

Also, remember that you want to keep the interview short but informative. The more you get your applicant talking, the more you can learn in a short amount of time. Open-ended questions are key.

When organizing your interview questions, it is best to use the "funnel" technique, in which general questions open the interview and are gradually replaced with more and more detailed questions. The more detailed the questions, the more you should focus on determining whether the applicant has the attributes you desire. You can finish the interview with yes-or-no questions as a way to confirm what you have learned. This is a tried-and-true interview technique that will really serve you well.

Once you have your job descriptions written, your model employees described, and the applications rolling in, it's time to do some real interviewing. In addition to using the funnel technique, you should try to organize your actual interview time according to the following parameters. First, introduce yourself and make friendly conversation with the applicant. This phase should last about three minutes and should serve to create a relaxed atmosphere in the interview room. Second, for about two minutes, inform the applicant that the interview will begin with some general questions; offer to allow the applicant to take notes but request that he or she save any questions for later; and make sure that the applicant is comfortable (perhaps offer a drink or a snack). Next, your question phase should follow and should last about 20 minutes. Use your prepared list as a guide and take notes, but do not hesitate to stray from your prepared list; if the applicant says something that you'd like to follow-up, do so. Just be sure that you cover all key points and find out as much as you need to know about the applicant's qualifications. Afterward, leave about 10 minutes for applicant questions. Be honest and answer questions as clearly and simply as possible. If the applicant asks a question that you are uncomfortable answering, say that it is against policy to discuss the issue. Once all questions are answered, conclude the phase by thanking the applicant. If you are convinced of their worthiness, offer the position. If not, tell them you will get back to them in a timely fashion.

While conducting your interview, it is of utmost importance to remember the many laws protecting the rights of applicants. You must abide by these laws at all times and avoid questions that could lead to potential allegations of discrimination. If you follow a few basic guidelines, you can interview at ease.

First, ask no questions that seem to target a specific group such as women, gay people, or ethnic minorities. For example, rather than asking if an employee has a college degree (which could be considered as discriminatory against ethnic groups with historically less opportunity for higher education), ask about the employee's level of education..

Second, only ask questions that directly relate to the position for which the applicant is interviewing. As long as your questions are pertinent to the job qualifications and requirements, you are within your bounds.

Third, remember the Americans with Disabilities Act. This law does not require that your hire disabled employees, but it does guard against you not hiring a disabled applicant if he or she could perform the job duties despite the disability. When interviewing a disabled person, first determine if reasonable accommodations could be made to allow that person to perform the job duties, and then focus on the person's qualifications as usual. Do not be afraid to ask the applicant what he or she will need to perform the job; in fact, we encourage you to do so. Stay positive.

BEING A GOOD BOSS

While you may succeed in hiring all the right employees, your efforts will have been in vain if you cannot manage your staff effectively. Your managerial style will be determined by your experience and personality and the type of business you are running.

If you are running a fast-food business, for example, your workers will probably be largely composed of part-time workers with little or no work experience. You will most likely not offer a benefits package or paid leave. Given these conditions, it will be important to have clear-cut rules and well-formulated guidelines for your employees to follow. Keeping your employees working smoothly will be your biggest challenge. In contrast, if you run a business with more skilled laborers, your employees will be seeking a greater degree of job satisfaction and might be planning long-term careers in the industry. For these workers, opportunity for growth and learning and the potential for investment in the company will be important incentives. Whatever your business, though, one thing remains the same. You are the boss. You are the role model, and you are the decision maker. Have high expectations and hold yourself to the same level; you will earn respect and have satisfied and hard-working employees.

Nevertheless, in the event that you have a less-than-stellar employee, you will need to take appropriate steps to solve the issue. Motivation is an important part of successful management, but so is taking steps to alleviate the factors that lead to a lack of employee motivation. You should provide each employee with a set of written rules of conduct and clearly outline the consequences of breaking each rule. Rules can be divided according to consequence. For example, state that breaking one set of rules will result in suspension, while breaking another set will result in termination. This will provide you with a fair way of correcting problem behavior.

Enforcing rules is as important as making them. You can write out all the rules you want, but if you don't back them up with action, your employees will not take them (or you) seriously. You must maintain consistent standards for your managerial strategies to work. You should tackle problems as soon as you notice them. Remember that  if you've noticed a problem, it's a big enough problem to be addressed. Be sure you are systematic and just, in case you need to defend your position in court; in other words, be clear in your expectations and intentions, deal with the problem as soon as it arises, base your actions on accepted guidelines, defend your position with documented facts, do not at any time disrespect the employee, and make sure that the punishment fits the infraction.

If you follow these simple suggestions, you should be able to maintain workplace consistency and deal successfully with most problems.

Buying and Managing Supplies

I f you are part of a large franchise, you are probably not alone when it comes to purchasing your supplies. Larger franchises often have a co-op system in place in which the purchases of different franchises and the franchiser are combined, saving time and money for everyone. In other cases you will need to order and maintain your own supplies, but even then, your franchiser will usually provide you with a list of approved or preferred providers. On occasion, you will have no purchasing requirements and can use whatever provider you choose. No matter which way you cut it, your purchasing should never be a shot in the dark.

Why would a franchiser provide a preferred list? For uniformity and quality. Franchisers want to maintain uniformity across franchises, and by using providers that are tested and true, they can be assured of the quality and consistency of the product franchises offer. This is an important factor in building brand recognition and trust among consumers.

You can check item six of your UFOC for information concerning the methods your franchiser expects you to use when purchasing. This section will also tell you if your franchiser receives referral income from the provider. The receipt of such income is not a problem and should not be frowned upon unless the extra cost to you is substantial. If you are trying to keep a tight ship financially, you might find that referral fees are raising the cost of supplies too much. However, weigh this against the relationship that the franchiser has built with the suppliers, which will directly benefit you.

You will rarely be required to purchase directly from the franchiser (one exception to this is if you work in a franchise with a "secret recipe" formula or some other proprietary substance). If your franchiser does distribute other types of supplies, they are probably not your only option, and you will usually be allowed to use your own suppliers. Of course, they will have to meet the standards for quality set by the franchiser. If your UFOC states that your supplies should all be purchased from the franchiser, be on the lookout for marked-up prices.

You may need to negotiate with your supplier for better prices. Never sacrifice quality. Keep your eye out for rebates, good deals, and trustworthy suppliers your franchiser may not know about. If you find such a supplier, don't keep it a secret — let the head office know about it.

GROUP PURCHASING

As mentioned in the beginning of the chapter, purchasing as a group will save you substantial amounts of time and money. Co-op purchasing groups can consist of individual franchisees, franchisees and the franchiser, or even different franchise systems working together to get a fair price. In addition to lower prices and better service, franchises in a co-op maybe have access to newer products sooner than those outside of a co-op.

Usually, a franchise can join a co-op by purchasing a membership and signing an agreement to buy a given percentage of all needed supplies through the co-op. The co-op often has a panel of officers voted in by the co-op members (one vote per store). Co-ops also may provide members with patronage dividends; the amount received per store is commensurate with the amount the store purchased through the co-op.

Joining a co-op might be a good idea for you, but never forget to maintain the standards set forth by your franchiser. Do not buy inferior products simply because they are available through the co-op.

LOCATING YOUR OWN SUPPLIERS

If you own a smaller franchise and are forced to locate your own providers without the benefit of an approved list from your franchiser, you will need to concentrate heavily on building strong relationships with your suppliers. This is also the case for franchises that need to purchase locally, for whatever reason.

To get started, ask the purchasing department of your franchiser for advice on suppliers in your locale. If not, check with your local chamber of commerce or with businesses similar to yours.

When approaching a supplier, you should already know your needs as well as any requirements set forth by your franchiser. You should also have prepared a list of quantities needed in order to avoid understocking or overstocking, which can hurt your wallet as much as your credibility. Finally, comparison shop before choosing a supplier. You should obtain and check references from each supplier, receive any bids in writing, and do a thorough analysis of their delivery schedules, product availability, pricing, and any additional fees charged (such as shipping and handling). Also, evaluate their level of customer service, standards for quality, knowledge about the products, and credit terms.

You should also look for a supplier with good service provided after delivery, not just before. Some providers, for instance, will offer detailed reports on your purchasing habits. As always, speak to other franchisees about the reputation of various suppliers. Ask your franchiser if they provide a standardized vendor evaluation form. These forms are a great way to organize your information and help you make an informed decision about which suppliers to use.

MANAGING YOUR SUPPLIES

Choosing good suppliers is half the battle. You must also be able to manage your stock of supplies in order to maintain a fluid flow of goods in and out of your store, and this involves interacting with your supplier to guarantee successful purchase and delivery.

Managing your stocked supplies begins with setting up a routine delivery schedule to prevent both overstocking or understocking. Often, suggested delivery schedules are provided by your franchiser. Whatever your schedule, be sure that deliveries occur during off-peak hours when the customer census is low. Only accept deliveries at these times, and only accept deliveries that you have scheduled. The driver should park in a place that won't inconvenience customers and should bring all merchandise into the store for you.

After an order is brought in, check to make sure that the order is meant for your store and that it is complete and matches the invoice (items in addition to quantity). Any substitutions should be verified with the franchiser. Ask for the delivery receipt immediately, and do not return it until the delivery is complete. If the supplier leaves with boxes, ensure that they are empty before they leave the store. Shelves should be checked before and after the supplier leaves. Perishables should be put away immediately and all boxes and containers should be checked thoroughly for damage. Check expiration dates to be sure the product will sell before it expires. Any problems should be noted on the receiving record, including damaged boxes or boxes appearing to have been resealed, as well as substitutions, missing items, and any other oddities. Have the driver sign the sheet before you do. Most importantly, don't be distracted. Focus, pay attention to the delivery, and make sure you get what you paid for.

ORGANIZING YOUR STOCKROOM

After you receive supplies, it is imperative to keep them well organized. Your stockroom will most likely be located in the back of the store, out of the way of customers, and will contain all inventory not in use or on the shelves. Some franchisers provide diagrams showing how stockrooms should be organized and maintained. All inventory should be stored according to regulation, and you should have an updated list of all supplies in your inventory at all times.

If your franchiser has not provided a diagram and storeroom organization is up to you, you can benefit by following these short tips.

Storing Dry Goods

- Store your inventory at least six inches from the floor. This makes cleaning easier and will protect your inventory from contamination and minor flooding.

- Store inventory away from sources of contamination, such as water lines. Poisonous materials, such as cleaning supplies, should be kept distant from consumable goods, such as food.

- Date and rotate all inventory, especially inventory with an expiration date.

- The heavier the product, the lower it should be stored to the ground. In addition, the more frequently needed the product, the closer to the storeroom entrance it should be stored.

- Keep the storeroom clean.

- Do not store any inventory above shoulder height to minimize employee injury and product damage.

Storing Perishables

Many of the same rules as above apply. Also take the following into account:

- Items needing refrigeration should be placed into refrigeration as soon as they are received.

- Any food removed from its original packaging should be repackaged and labeled right away.

- All temperatures should be checked daily. In addition, freezers, refrigerators, thermostats, and other storage devices should be checked and maintained regularly, and any and all regulations followed precisely.

Organizing Your Shelves

Outside of the stockroom is your store, which customers see on a daily basis. Clean and well-organized shelves and product presentation are key to attracting and keeping customers.

- Keep the shelves stocked. Empty shelves are unimpressive and unattractive.

- Keep stock rotated on the shelves in the store (as well as in the storeroom).

- Maintain consistent pricing.

- Keep any signage up to date and only use signage approved by your franchiser.

- Follow all regulations applying to shelving.

- Keep the store neat and clean.

- Make sure your store complies with the Americans with Disabilities Act. Allow enough room between aisles for the disabled to browse your shelves, keep things within easy reach, and train your staff to help disabled customers.

Managing Supplier and Franchiser Relationships

In running a franchise you have a number of allies: your franchiser, their partners, and your fellow franchisees. The success of one will result in increased success for the others, and so these relationships should be nourished and maintained with strong two-way communication. You will see that as individual franchises grow and do better, the parent company will grow, and the name and trademarks of the company will increase in recognition and reputation. This will equate to more customers and increased revenue for you and everyone else involved in the franchise system.

COMMUNICATION

As we have stated time and again, your best sources of information are your fellow franchisees and your franchiser. In this chapter we would like to emphasize that these are great sources for your success. Franchisees who have been in the game for some time know the system and can help you succeed by offering advice and guidance. Their reward is your own success, because when you succeed and build a reputation in the community, they will also reap the benefits. It is important to develop and maintain exceptional communication with these resources. A two-way information flow is best: as they share information and advice with you, you will share it with them, and everyone will benefit and prosper.

If you own a franchise within a smaller organization (say, less than about 40 stores), you will most likely be in frequent communication directly with the owner of the franchise. In small systems the business plan is often still being developed and changed. If you maintain steady communication with the owner, you will benefit from receiving up-to-date information on any changes or developments. The owner will also benefit from hearing about problems you are encountering, even those specific to your area and demographic. Your input can lead to a better business model for all the franchisees in the system, and this will lead to a stronger system overall.

If you own a franchise within a mid-sized organization (40–100 stores), rather than communicating frequently with the owner, you will probably find yourself in frequent communication with the owner's representative or with a leading franchisee. Again, your feedback exchanged for their experience and advice will create a loop of information that can be used to improve the system for all.

For owners of a franchise in a large organization (more than 100 stores) it will support and back you up at all times. You will probably be assigned a representative or regional manager, with whom you should maintain frequent two-way communication. All the benefits of communication that apply to small- and mid-sized organizations also apply to larger organizations.

No matter what size franchise you are a part of, remember to get to know your representative or owner, ask for and follow advice, and provide feedback. If you ignore the advice of others, the advice will soon stop coming. Likewise, if you do not contribute to the information flow with feedback, you might soon be left out of the loop. You do not want to be viewed as a whiner, complainer, or troublemaker who does not offer solutions to problems. Rather, you want to be viewed as a productive member of the team. Offer help when others need it, and you will be offered help when you need it. Offer advice and feedback to others, and you will receive the same in return.

Remember that your representative will want to see you meet certain requirements and that no amount of good faith between the two of you will change these requirements. For instance, it is your responsibility to ensure that your business operates according to the standards set forth by the franchiser. Your adherence to these standards might be evaluated by surprise visits from the representative or by evaluations collected from "undercover" shoppers (franchiser employees entering your store to evaluate your performance). You will be required to correct any procedural or compliance problems. Do not mistake your positive working relationship with your franchiser or representative as free reign to do whatever you want. You are still a part of the system, and you must remain cooperative and true to the system's vision at all times.

MAKING YOUR CONTRIBUTION TO THE SUCCESS OF THE FRANCHISE

Along with trust and respect comes additional opportunity. If your franchiser feels that you have been a productive member of the team, offering advice and help, providing feedback, and maintaining positive communication, you may be offered additional responsibilities or duties, such as helping new franchisees or evaluating new products. Whatever the compensation, such opportunities can do much to improve your bottom line. They are functions necessary to make your franchise system grow as a whole. This growth will cause your own business to expand and become more reputable and trustworthy.

Asking a franchisee to perform these duties is far more desirable than hiring an outsider for several reasons. First, outside consultants can be costly. Second, they are unfamiliar with the detailed workings of the system. Third, hiring an outsider risks exposing trade secrets or other information that the system has a vested interest in keeping hidden from general knowledge. Fourth, the consultant does not have personal interest in the overall success of the franchise system. Having selected franchisees take on extra responsibility for the health and growth of the system is far superior than outsourcing. If offered the opportunity to assume these extra capabilities, take it.

New Products

One task you might be asked to tackle is testing new products before they are distributed to the entire franchise system. Because the introduction of a new product takes a great investment, this is a very important task. You will be part of the team that decides whether the new product will be likely to be profitable despite advertising, training, signage, new packaging, and the other costs associated with it. A new product may bring many new customers to your location during the trial and to all the franchises once it is introduced more widely.

Your successful promotion of a new product will highlight your worth to your franchiser. If the product fails, do not worry. You will have gained new customers, and the failure of the product will have no financial impact on you. Rather, costs associated with the product will be borne by the franchiser.

New Procedures

In addition to new products, you might be asked to help evaluate new procedures. Your employees will be heavily involved in the testing. You should be sure to emphasize to them that this is just a test and that any and all feedback is welcome. Your employees could be key to helping the system accept, modify, or reject the procedure. At the conclusion of the test period you should add your own feedback comments to those of your employees and submit an honest opinion of the procedure. Discuss both the good and bad aspects and suggest areas for improvement. It is important to be honest; you do not want the franchiser to put a faulty procedure in place based upon your positive recommendation.

Training Assistance

After the establishment of a new franchise the franchiser will often provide aid for a set number of days. If you are successful and respected by the franchiser, you might be asked to serve as a training assistant, providing advice and guidance to new franchisees after the initial training period has expired. You could also volunteer to help. If you are asked to help, you will know that your franchiser has noticed your success and enthusiasm. If you volunteer, you will demonstrate your willingness to be a part of the team. Either situation will earn you respect and recognition from the franchiser and other franchisees.

Be sure to bring along your own training materials, which should be extensively annotated with your thoughts and suggestions. Also, remember to offer compliments on the things that the new franchisee is doing correctly; don't just focus on the negative. This will give the new franchisee a much-needed confidence boost. At the same time, do not try to spare the franchisee's feelings by ignoring some bad behaviors or methods. Be sure to point out all mistakes so that they can be corrected. In other words, point out all the problems while also complimenting all the successes. Finally, know when your job is done. Give the new franchisee advice, and let them work their business. You do not want to become too involved. This will make the new franchisee dependent on you and will also take up time and energy you need for your own business.

Selling the Business

Franchise systems are similar to many other programs in that you might be offered an award if you refer another person to the franchise. This award may come in the form of a commission or royalty. If you know that your company has such a policy, it is in your best interest to take advantage of it. Making successful referrals is a lot easier than you might think. If your franchise does not sponsor referral awards, make referrals anyway. Remember, if you do all you can do to help your franchise system grow, you will reap the benefits.

The simplest way to go about finding referrals is to talk about your business. You will find that the more successful and happy you are with your progress, the more friends, family, and acquaintances will want to know. If they see that you are satisfied, enjoying yourself, and making money, many people will ask how they can get involved. This is especially true if you began with no business background or unique product; they will see that franchising makes sense for anyone who wants to run a small business but doesn't know where, when, or how to start.

You should begin to communicate frequently with anyone who expresses a serious interest in franchising. Answer all their questions and suggest that they come and take a small tour of your business. When and if they are ready to learn more, make a personal referral to your owner or representative (with whom you should be keeping in frequent contact).

IMPROVING EFFICIENCY

You can do your part to help improve the efficiency of the procedures in your franchise system. For example, if you find that doing something by the book does not produce satisfactory results, you are not within your right as a franchisee to change the procedure. Rather, consult with other franchisees and determine whether they are experiencing similar problems. If they are not, find out what you might be doing wrong. If they are, you have found an inefficient procedure that needs amendment. Tell your representative about the details of the procedure, why it isn't working, and ways it could be improved. It would not hurt to also put the entire problem into writing for further review.

While the amended procedure will need to be tested before its implementation, your franchiser's respect for you will grow because of your contribution to the success of the system as a whole.

VENDOR AND CONSULTANT RELATIONSHIPS

In addition to maintaining good relationships with your franchiser and other franchisees, it is important to nurture your relationship with vendors. Vendors or suppliers are usually under contract to the franchiser to provide supplies to all franchisees, so your personal relationship with them is vastly important. While vendors are typically working under a tight schedule and within a set budget, with the right communication skills you might be able to ask for small modifications to their procedures to better serve you. In other words, if you maintain a good working relationship with your vendors, they will do all they can to help you.

Your franchiser might also employ business consultants. Their task is to get to know the operation and provide useful suggestions to increase efficiency. You might be asked to play host to a consultant by giving him or her a tour of your operations. You should cooperate and communicate honestly with all consultants; their job is to make improvements to the franchise system, which will also improve your own business. Remember that the cost of consultants is very high, so put them to good use and give them all the information they need to make productive decisions.

Working with Your Fellow Franchisees

Your fellow franchisees are important allies to the success of your business. Stay in touch with them and be a part of the team, and you will reap numerous rewards.

You may find that the franchisees in your area hold meetings at which they discuss the business. Become a part of these meetings. If you do your share, you will be a welcome member of the group. If such meetings are not taking place, why not organize them yourself? Don't worry about setting an agenda. You will find that there will be plenty of conversation without one.

The franchisees in your area might also be participating in, or willing to participate in, joint advertising ventures. They might also collectively sponsor children's sports teams or contribute to charitable organizations. Group advertising saves time and money for everyone involved. In addition, being part of a group can help you in less obvious ways. For example, good relationships with your fellow franchisees may result in their helping you with large or difficult orders or procedures, referring additional customers to you, or providing resources when it's time for you to take that well-earned vacation.

Community Relations

Being a part of your community as a whole will earn you a good reputation and more customers. You want to be a contributing part of your community.

In addition to sponsoring local teams or giving to local charities, try joining a community service group such as the Rotary Club or Lion's Club. This is a great way to take part in community improvement, while at the same time making a name for your business. In the same vein, be sure to attend meetings of your local chamber of commerce and take an active role in the business community in your area.

While participating in community events, you should shy away from causes or events such as political races and endorsements that might alienate your business from certain segments of the community population. An easy way to avoid invitations for events such as political breakfast is to say that it is against your policy.

OUTSIDE RESOURCES

In many cases, there will be aspects of your business that you might need to outsource if you do not have the time or skill to do them yourself. Unless you are already proficient in accounting and tax law, you might need to hire an outside accountant to manage both your business and personal accounts.

Your advertising and marketing might best be served by the

expertise of professionals. While you expect branding and large-scale advertising to be managed by the franchiser, you will still need to make people aware of your individual location, and so local advertising will be up to you. To take it to the next level, a marketing agent can help you launch a full-scale campaign, including television, radio, and cable marketing.

Maintaining good relationships with these professionals is vital. You want them to do the best job for you that they can, and this is more likely to happen with open, honest, professional, and frequent two-way communication.

EMPLOYEE RELATIONS

Do not forget about your employees! They are your most important investment. You can have a clean, attractive, well-stocked store within the framework of a reputable and profitable franchise system, but unhappy employees will result in unhappy customers. Offer incentives, rewards, and recognition for a job well done. Be fair and equitable in your treatment. You should consider creating an anonymous feedback program that will allow you to filter employee complaints and pinpoint emerging issues before they become problems.

HANDLING STRESS AND MAKING COMPLAINTS

At this point you may be thinking how you are expected to maintain a positive relationship with all these entities while also dealing with the inevitable stress and problems of running your own business. Don't worry! There are methods you can use to deal with negative issues while also maintaining positive relationships.

Dealing with Stress (Without Making Enemies)

Stress is two-pronged. It can work to your advantage by forcing you to accomplish your goals as necessary to succeed, or it can get the best of you and ruin your personal relationships, health, and your business. To run a small business, you must be able to make stress work for you. Being the cool and collected one in a group of stressed-out fellow franchisees will earn you a reputation for leadership. Above all, taking the inevitable stress and turning it into efficiency and profit will help your business grow in leaps and bounds.

You can control your levels of stress by (1) planning ahead for the stress, (2) calling for help, (3) controlling your breathing, and (4) taking breaks. Know when stressful times are coming and prepare for them. Get smaller jobs out of the way early to leave plenty of time for bigger jobs. If you need help, ask for it. Don't be afraid to call upon your fellow franchisees or your franchiser. Finally, on a more personal level, learn helpful breathing techniques to keep you calm, and take frequent breaks from difficult tasks in order to clear your mind and prevent anxiety.

Making Complaints (Nicely)

You might encounter a problem in the operation of your business or your franchise system as a whole that you cannot solve yourself. In these cases you might be forced to file a formal complaint. Remember when doing so that your complaint will help the franchise system as a whole operate more smoothly, so don't feel like a snitch.

When lodging a complaint, remember to operate according to the chain of command. Go first to your direct superior. Do not go above him or her unless the complaint is about him or her. Doing so will only hurt the relationship you have carefully fostered with your representative.

If possible, try to lodge the complaint in person. Organize a meeting time and place that is convenient to both of you. If possible, arrange a meeting place and time that will allow you to demonstrate the problem at hand. Begin the meeting with positives: talk about your business and its successes, ask about the successes of the franchise as a whole, and offer thanks for the help your representative has given you. This will set a positive tone and will make your representative more open to listening to your complaint. Then, discuss the issue. Don't be surprised if the representative is already aware of it and can offer immediate advice on how to rectify it.

Dealing with Bad News

If you find your business heading in the wrong direction, alert your representative. Do not try to hide bad news. Addressing the problem will often lead to a good solution while ignoring problems can surely lead to your downfall. You will not have been the only franchisee to need some guidance and help, so don't feel ashamed or embarrassed. Part of being a business owner is acknowledging when things are going wrong and seeking help.

Take all the advice you can get. If your representative devises a plan, follow it carefully and do not deviate from it at all. Depend upon his or her expertise to get you out of tough situations. Most importantly, keep communication flowing. Your representative is on your side and wants success for you as much as you do.

Cost Control

Learning ways to control cost is important. This short chapter will provide you with some useful tips for doing just that. Remember that while you will have little to no control over your revenue, you will have great control over your costs. Your profit depends on the difference between the two, so controlling costs will allow you a little more breathing room when it comes to revenue.

First, create a daily budget and consult it. Do not depend upon checking your budget weekly, monthly, or quarterly. Successful budgeting entails frequent tweaks. Getting to know your budget on a daily basis will help you decide where spending is necessary, where it is extraneous, and whether you are meeting or exceeding predicted costs. Your budget should be a living document that is updated frequently.

To keep accurate records and better control of costs, create detailed categories for your expense reports rather than broad categories. For example, rather than creating an "office supplies" category, create categories for "paper," "postage," "ink," "equipment repairs," and so on. You may find room for improvement in these smaller areas that would have been unnoticeable in broader categories.

Seriously consider asking your store manager to keep track of the store budget. This will increase his or her sense of responsibility and will cause him or her to be more focused on meeting store goals. You can even offer incentives to encourage managers to meet store goals under budget.

While effective cost control will help keep your business healthy, remember that it is possible to take cost control too far. Don't skimp on the essentials. For instance, you must keep your equipment up to par with scheduled maintenance checks. If you fail to do so, you will find that repairs and lost time end up costing much more than responsible maintenance would have.

Finally, if your franchise is a restaurant, it is a good idea to invest in a manual devoted to food service cost controls. Check out *The Food Service Manager's Guide to Creative Cost Cutting: Over 2001 Innovative and Simple Ways to Save Your Food Service Operation Thousands by Reducing Expenses*, available from Atlantic Publishing for $79.95, Item #CCC-01. Call (800) 814-1132 or order online at **www.atlantic-pub.com**.

CHAPTER

14

Territorial Strategies

Territorial rules and limitations, if you own a franchise with territorial concerns, are things that your franchiser will have thought out and set up for you. You should be aware of how territorial conditions are arranged and understand how they are formed by your franchiser. Three considerations must be taken into account: (1) whether multi-unit franchising is an option, (2) how territories should be made up, and (3) whether franchisees should be allowed to expand their existing territories.

MULTI-UNIT FRANCHISING

A franchiser needs to decide whether one or multiple units will be made available for sale to a single franchisee. Multi-unit franchising can take one of three forms, which are outlined and described below.

Master Franchising

In this system the franchiser sells a master franchisee the right to recruit and train other franchisees in exchange for royalty payments or a portion of the franchise fees collected from these additional franchisees. This arrangement is great for the growth of the franchise system in that it reduces the franchiser's overhead by cutting down on permanent headquarters staff and reduces conflict caused by excessive market growth. In addition, master franchising makes buyback easier by reducing the number of people with whom the franchiser must deal during the buyback of a unit.

When knowledge of a particular market or locale is needed, master franchising is great because the franchiser is able to work with someone established in that market. This is particularly beneficial when a franchiser is looking to expand internationally, as the master franchiser will be familiar with local customs and currency and able to judge the worthiness of potential franchisees in that region or country.

Master franchising does have its drawbacks. First, new franchisees lose some of their incentive for success because they do not hold an exclusive contract. Second, master franchising makes quality control much more difficult (for the same reasons). In addition, the selection of a single bad franchisee can inflict serious damage on the system as a whole.

Area Development

In this system a franchisee is given the right to a large area with the potential to host more than one outlet. The area is thus given to the franchisee for development. This system puts a stop to the piggybacking of individually owned franchises in a single area on one another's advertising efforts and reduces the total number of franchisees to manage. In addition, this system requires less training and development on the part of the franchiser as not every newly opened outlet needs guidance, information, and starting materials.

On the other hand, the franchiser loses some incentives in starting such a system. For example, individual franchisees realize increased power over the franchiser.

Subfranchising

In this system the franchiser permits certain franchisees to sell new franchises and becoming subfranchisers who are responsible for training and development and entitled to collect royalties from the subfranchisees.

This system is great for quicker growth and requires fewer employees at headquarters. However, conflicts between the franchiser and subfranchisers may arise over such issues as the schedule of system development and the ability of subfranchisers to recruit new franchisees in a time frame desired by the franchiser. In addition, the franchiser loses some power because subfranchisers have a great deal more power than regular franchisees. Also, choosing new subfranchisers is difficult given the relatively small number of people with enough capital to become a subfranchiser.

TERRITORY DIVISIONS

Exclusivity is an important feature of territory formation. Although guaranteeing exclusive territory rights to franchisees usually results in a reduced amount of market saturation, it is still a great strategy to use for certain products or for new franchise systems. Statistics have shown that of the 170 new franchise systems begun in the 1990s, 91 percent of the surviving systems use exclusive territories.

As suggested by the concept of area development, exclusive territories cut down on the practice of some franchises exploiting the advertising efforts of other franchises in the same area. In addition, franchisees with exclusive territory rights need not worry about excessive competition from other franchisees or the franchiser.

Exclusive territories are generally small. The franchiser wants to offer the benefits of exclusive territories without diminishing market saturation to such a degree that the franchise system as a whole suffers. Without enough franchises in the marketplace, competing franchises will gain a better position. Territories must be small enough to allow healthy competition while also sheltering franchisees against encroachment. Territories can be allotted based on population, wealth, or other demographic factors—not on an equality of geographic size.

RIGHT TO EXPAND

Whether or not franchisees have the right to expand their territories is a final factor that must be weighed and considered by a franchiser. Allowing expansion has many benefits. It gives franchisees a greater incentive to succeed and conform to the franchise system's strategies and rules, making franchisees much easier to monitor. The incentive lies in the fact that most expansions are permitted based upon the success level of the franchisee. In addition, allowing franchisees to expand cuts costs for the franchiser because it costs less to expand than to open a new outlet. From the perspective of the franchisee, expansion eliminates fears of encroachment and makes saturation problems disappear because they are in control of all outlets within their territory.

Expansion is covered in more detail in the following chapter.

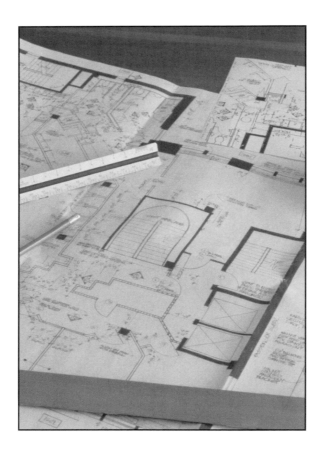

CHAPTER

15

Expanding Your Operations

or you, owning one franchise might be enough. On the other hand, you might be the kind of person who wants to own and run more than one outlet. In this chapter, you will find the information and guidance to help you determine whether you are cut out for multiple franchise ownership — legally, financially, and personally. We will also discuss the negative and positive aspects of owning more than one franchise.

CHECKING YOUR FRANCHISE AGREEMENT: CAN YOU BUY ANOTHER FRANCHISE?

Before you can own multiple units, you need to make sure that multi-unit ownership is permissible under. If multi-unit ownership is an option, learn all you can about the restrictions governing it. You want to remain in compliance with your agreement at all times. This information might be included in the UFOC. If it's not, a simple query to your franchiser will provide all the information you need. Make sure to ask about franchise fees and royalties for multiple units. Fees will probably be lower for expansion units than for the original unit, but double check to be sure.

Transfers might be permitted, but your agreement may state that the franchiser has the right to reject proposed transfers. If your current location is not functioning up to the franchiser's standards, a rejection is possible. In addition, the franchiser may have the right of first refusal for any franchise that comes onto the market.

UNDERSTANDING YOUR PURCHASE OPTIONS

If there are no restrictions on the establishment of an additional franchise, you will need to decide where, when, and how to set up shop. You will need to evaluate sites for your new franchise in the same way you did for your original franchise, considering traffic, demographics, lease terms, competition, and building costs.

Buying an Existing Franchise

You might have your eye on a neighbor's business. Even if it seems as though the franchise is happy and successful, he or she might be ready to leave the business for any number of reasons. You'll never know until you inquire. Once again, communication with your fellow franchisees could alert you to businesses that will soon be for sale or that could be for sale if you express an interest.

You should try to learn about the sales status of existing franchises from your franchiser. Once they know about your plans to expand, they could suggest an existing franchise for you to take over, or you can ask them about any that might be up for sale about which they know and you don't. Your franchiser might even sponsor an active resale network. They would rather see existing franchises taken over by willing owners than see them close completely.

If you find a potential location to take over, you will need to scrutinize it carefully to make sure it will be right for you. The location should be close enough to your original location that you can easily keep tabs on both, but far enough away to avoid competition with your current location. You should figure out why the current owners are willing to sell. If they are selling for personal reasons, that's one thing, but if they are selling because there are problems with the store, you will need to address those problems and determine whether they can be solved.

You should insist on seeing the performance statistics of any unit you are thinking of purchasing. You can ask either your franchiser or the franchisee for operating figures and results. Since you already know the business well and you have experience running a successful unit, you should be able to analyze these numbers and decide whether the business will be profitable for you.

When considering the purchase of an existing franchise, you should answer the following questions:

- Does the current location meet the franchise system's standards? One of the benefits of buying an existing franchise is that the equipment should already be there and the building itself should be ready to go. If the location is not quite up to par, weigh the expenses of improvements against the expense of building a new location, and go from there.

- How profitable is the existing franchise? Can any problems be solved?

- Does the original franchise contract have enough years remaining on it to allow you to amortize your additional costs?

- Has the franchiser assigned the location good reviews in the past?

- What are the current employees like? Will they be willing to continue working at the location after a transfer of ownership? Can you resolve any current labor conflicts? Are the managers reliable and trustworthy? Will the managers at your current location be willing to transfer, if necessary?

- What does the public think about the location? If the public's opinion is low, can steps be taken to regain trust and customers? Do current demographics of the area still match your target-customer profile, or has the demographic landscape changed with time?

- What are the terms of the current lease, and do they meet your interests?

- Are there existing legal problems that could affect you in the future?

- Does the location pass all standards you would set for a new location?

RETRO-FRANCHISING

Through retro-franchising you might have the opportunity to buy a location directly from your franchiser. Many franchisers own and operate their own locations; some of these were set up for the long term, and others were set up with the intention of selling them to franchisees at a later date. Your franchiser might be willing to sell you a company-owned location for a number of reasons—to cut losses, expand markets, increase capital, or simply because the location was created just for that purpose.

At times a franchiser has an opportunity to purchase space that will serve as a great location in the future. For example, a new subway station might be built with room for a restaurant, and a restaurant franchiser might purchase that slot with the intention of finding someone to run the location at a later date. These could present great opportunities for you, although many of these locations are nontraditional.

Franchisers take into account the concept of "critical mass" when considering whether to sell a location to a franchisee. Critical mass is simply the number of units deemed necessary to infiltrate a market area. This allows efficient advertising and increases brand recognition within these markets. Also, when an area reaches critical mass, the franchiser is able to provide better support for existing franchises by sending field agents out to more units at a lower total cost. Your franchiser may be willing to sell you a location to get closer to critical mass in a given market.

Retro-franchising is a great option because you will acquire a store that is already running and is up to standards. In addition, franchisers will sometimes sell these units at a discounted price. Our only caution to you is to beware of "churning." This is a practice in which a franchiser will sell a location to a franchisee and then take it back with the intention of selling again, knowing that every franchisee is destined to fail at that location due to unavoidable problems. Check the history of any location you are considering retro-franchising.

CONVERTING A COMPETITOR'S LOCATION

If you would like to take over an existing establishment but cannot find any opportunities in your desired market within your own franchise system, you might want to consider taking over a competitor's location. If you find a suitable location that meets your needs and is up for sale, you can both expand your business and reduce your competition in one move.

Independent mom-and-pop businesses are finding it more difficult to compete with franchises in the same market. If you ask around, you might be able to purchase a location from one of these independents. Since you are operating in the same industry, you will benefit from an existing customer pool, and, while employees will need to be trained, they may be willing to stay and work for you.

Taking over a competitor's location will entail substantial remodeling. Zoning issues should not come into play. You will need to hire a contractor to complete any restructuring, and you might need to invest in equipment that meets your franchise system's standards. It costs less to remodel than to build a new location.

In certain situations, such as when extensive plumbing, electrical, or structural changes are required, it might be easier and cheaper to build a new location. You should check with your franchiser's development department to determine the costs of each move.

You will also need to check with a lawyer to go over the franchise agreements of your franchiser and the franchiser of the original owner, if applicable. The original franchisee might have signed an agreement preventing their selling the location to a competitor. You should also make sure that by purchasing the new location you are not violating the territorial rights of another franchisee within your system.

STARTING FROM SCRATCH

Don't forget that if you cannot locate a suitable existing location, you always have the option of starting from scratch and repeating the steps you took to select and prepare your first location.

BUYING MULTIPLE UNITS

While some franchisees decide to expand after experiencing success with their first business, you might have purchased your franchise with the intent to expand right from the beginning. You are not alone. Many franchisees are part of an investor group looking to open up multiple locations and get an inside edge on a market. Some of these groups could even be larger and more powerful than the franchiser. After the purchase of a handful of units you will probably find that you need to establish your own management facilities to coordinate the management of all your units. You might also need to establish training centers in order to accommodate the constant influx of new employees. Managers will have greater responsibility and will need training similar to that provided to the franchisees.

Acquiring an Area

If you have your sights set on multiple ownership from the beginning, you should find out if your franchiser offers the right to develop an area. You can purchase this right, and it will permit you to expand within a certain territory at an established rate (a certain number of units in a certain amount of time). Some franchise systems only allow expansion along this model. This way, the franchise systems minimize management and training needs, while simultaneously growing. Alternatively, your franchiser might offer area development expansion only within large, core markets; in smaller markets, your franchiser might only sell to individual franchisees who want to own one business.

Before you purchase area development rights, consider the following: (1) how many stores would you like to own?, (2) what is your financial situation, and will you be able to support your desired number of units?, (3) will the area being offered for development be able to support your desired number of units? and (4) what costs or savings will you see based on your decision to develop an area as opposed to over-purchasing additional units when they become available?

Do not enter into an area development agreement without substantial funds. You can expect to pay a huge up-front fee or a fee per franchise. Either way, the cost to you will most likely be large. You will, at the very least, be expected to pay the full franchise fee for the first unit along with a large percentage up-front deposit for each additional expected unit, with the remainder of the fee due upon the opening of each unit.

Keep in mind that if you do not end up opening the additional units, for whatever reason, you cannot necessarily expect your deposit back from the franchiser. You will also be expected to keep up with set development schedules. You should check on your franchiser's default policy before investing in area development. While financial policies are often in place, many franchisers will adapt their responses to late development according to individual circumstances. A fee could be assessed, or you might be granted a grace period. The franchiser will likely evaluate your degree of commitment to the project before determining the consequences of your default.

REVIEWING YOUR PERSONAL AND BUSINESS RESOURCES

After reading this chapter you might find yourself contemplating becoming a multi-unit owner. You need to perform some serious and honest personal and financial reflection before making any multi-unit commitments. When you add units, the entire structure and functioning of your business changes. You will find yourself operating on an entirely different scale. This can be a blessing or a curse. A good first bit of advice is to get your ideas, plans, and tactics out on paper. Often, the numbers, notes, and options you jot down will help you to visualize your situation more clearly and will help you to make the right decision.

Take Some Time for Personal Reflection

Before considering whether your business is ready for expansion you should determine if you are up to the task on a personal level. Remember that along with multiple ownership comes more frequent and required relationships. Ask yourself if you are ready to be in charge of a large team.

Your responsibilities will also increase dramatically. If you are currently struggling to get through the day — opening, operating, and closing up your business, while also maintaining a healthy personal life — then multiple ownership is probably not for you: imagine needing to manage the daily operations of two, three, or even 20 units! Or, alternatively, imagine managing the number of people it will take to oversee daily operations on your behalf. If your personal life is too demanding, then multiple ownership, at least at this time, is probably not right for you.

Since you cannot be everywhere at once, you will need to hire and manage reliable employees so that you can delegate authority. At the start of this new venture, you will probably focus on the new units, but eventually you will need to address the issues of all units. You will need to be able to entrust individual unit managers with many responsibilities.

You will need the organizational skills necessary to set up staff training and administration centers if you plan to operate more than a handful of units. These centers will need competent clerical, legal, and financial personnel.

Remember: the desire to expand is not enough. You must be personally capable of the expansion as well.

Take a Hard Look at Your Business and Finances

Before expanding, look at the current state of your finances and the health of your business. You did a lot of preparation before purchasing your first franchise unit. Did you prepare well? Did you make the right decisions? Before you purchase your next unit, think about the following.

- Are your employees ready to meet the demands an expansion will require? Look at your management. As a single store owner, you might serve as the general manager, with shift managers overseeing your employees directly. However, if you purchase additional units, you will need to manage all of the units as a whole, and give more responsibility to your shift managers. Are they able to become general managers? Are your other employees ready for new responsibility, and can you trust all your employees to operate the store without your constant presence?

- Before you invest time and money into expansion, take a look at the competitor landscape. If you are having problems keeping up with your competitors and want to expand to get a leg up, make sure they do not also have expansion plans. It would be a bad move to expand only to be shut down by a similar move by the competition.

- How will expansion affect your customer base? Will the loss of a personal touch be felt by loyal customers, or will expansion fit the needs of more of customers in other ways?

- Do you have the finances to expand? What fees and other costs will you be expected to pay in addition to the funds needed to open the new unit?

Crunching the Numbers

Whatever you do, you do not want the opening of a new unit to damage the success of a current unit, financially or otherwise. You should thoroughly examine your financial picture to ensure that this will not happen. Use your up-to-date balance sheets, investment portfolios, budgets, profit-and-loss statements, and cash flow analyses to make sure there are current sources of funding for the new unit. You might be able to make the numbers work by seeking out additional financing, perhaps even from your franchiser. Don't overburden yourself with debt to the point that both units suffer. Rates or loan policies may have changed since you took out the loan for your original unit. Costs of construction, licensure, or real estate may also have changed. For that matter, changing franchise agreements could make your startup costs higher than they were originally, despite the possibility of a reduced franchise fee for multiple ownership. Make sure you do your calculations based on current rates.

Don't forget that with more units to stock and maintain you will be purchasing more supplies. You might be able to get supplies at better cost through volume purchasing. Financial burdens as well as blessings should be taken into account when determining if you are financially ready to expand.

Finally, it is highly recommended that you turn to your legal, financial, and marketing professionals before committing to any expansion plans. They may provide you with insights that you missed during your own review. They may also be able to provide useful tips and advice. Discuss any plans with your franchiser's development staff as well.

THE PROS AND CONS
OF MULTIPLE OWNERSHIP

If you find yourself looking in the mirror in the morning thinking what a great guy or gal you are for being such a success, if your bank, franchiser, accountant, employees, and community all love you and congratulate you on a job well done, if you are planning to kick back and enjoy that dream vacation to Maui; if you are even planning on cashing in by opening more units—STOP! Do not think that your success as an individual franchise owner will carry over to multiple franchises. Multiple ownership has its pros and cons. We discuss these in this section. Weigh them carefully.

Pros

Opening more units could bring you more money. At the same time, you will be building equity in your businesses and in any real estate you purchase for your businesses. More units could mean cheaper costs in terms of supplies and employee benefits. In addition, you could receive better rates when you apply for loans and other financing.

Additional units also make the cost of marketing more palatable. You might have difficulty justifying the high cost of radio or television advertising for one unit, but when you are paying to promote multiple units, the advantages could easily outweigh the costs. More media exposure means more customers.

The larger your operations within a particular market, the more qualified employees you will attract. You will have the capability to offer more career development opportunities, and employees will have an easier time imagining such opportunities. In addition, you will no longer need to turn away as many qualified applicants because you will have more positions to fill. You will also be able to transfer staff from unit to unit, as need dictates, within the same market. This allows you and your employees much greater flexibility.

Finally, if pricing is not determined by your franchiser, you will be able to standardize pricing on identical products within your market (as opposed to having customers notice price differences between individually owned franchise units within the same area). This will lead to greater customer satisfaction by cutting down on confusion.

Cons

If you are not personally and financially prepared, opening multiple units could ruin your successful original unit. You will need the leadership, management skills, and capital to run multiple businesses. For some the old saying, "If it ain't broke, don't fix it," might apply. If you're not ready to expand, and you do it anyway, you could ruin a good thing.

You might think that with the hiring and training of management staff with more responsibility you will not have to take as much of a personal interest in the daily operations of your units. This assumption should be entirely avoided; it's a common pitfall.

Your success as a multi-unit owner may cause you to discover problems and flaws with the organization and practices of the franchise system, and you may be tempted to institute your own changes within your units—but you cannot. You must remember that no matter how large you grow, you are still a franchisee, and there are still rules to follow. This can be very frustrating.

You can easily turn these negatives into positives with the right thinking and the right approach. We leave you, once again, with the following advice: proceed only if you are ready!

Advantages and Disadvantages of the Franchise Model

16

I f you have a business you are thinking of franchising, this chapter is important. In it we will discuss the advantages and disadvantages of the franchise model. You should use this chapter to help decide whether franchising your own business is a step you should take.

When you own a business, one of the most important decisions you will need to make is how to organize management. Sole proprietorships give you all the control, and changes can be implemented in the blink of an eye. However, you may lack the range of talent that larger management systems can provide. Large corporations have the necessary talent, but change is difficult and takes time. Pyramid-shaped organizations function well at the top, but at the bottom levels you will often find that the organization is no longer in touch with its customer base. The lesson learned? No matter what organization you use for your company, it will have advantages and disadvantages. The key is to decide which organization is best suited to your company and which will give you the advantages you most need within your industry. One of the methods of organization to consider is franchising. It too has advantages and disadvantages.

ADVANTAGES

There are four basic advantages to the franchise model:

1. You take on a relatively low amount of risk for your financial returns.

2. Each store in and of itself will realize better incentives for success.

3. You will be able to attract better management talent.

4. You will experience an increased rate of growth over other models.

We discuss each of these benefits in the following sections.

Low Risk For Financial Returns

In franchising you are distributing risk among the various franchisees rather than holding all the cards in your own hand. Any failed expansions or other failed efforts for improvement are funded from the franchisees' pockets, not yours. In addition, you, as the franchiser, will also be able to assume more risk than otherwise possible. If you owned each outlet, you would want to have a very high chance of success at a particular location before paying to build a unit there. By franchising, this risk is partly assumed by the franchisee, and thus locations that are less than optimal can be developed for potential use.

Better Incentives For Success At The Unit Level

The best way to understand this benefit is to imagine the differences in managerial style between two managers, one corporate, one a franchisee. Imagine that Manager A works at a company-owned store with about $800,000 in sales per year. Manager A receives a salary of $55,000 plus the possibility of a bonus, which is based upon his sales and his ability to operate under budget. Most years, he does not get a bonus. Manager B, on the other hand, is a franchisee. Her store also does around $800,000 in sales annually. Rather than earning a set salary, Manager B takes the profit of the store minus expenses and royalty payments. At the end of the year she ends up taking home about the same amount as Manager A: $55,000.

Suppose both managers learn about a new food handling technique which, if implemented properly, will cut costs by about $10,000. The only cost to them will be about 10 hours of their time, required to train employees in this new procedure. If the managers decide to undertake the training, Manager A, because of his bonus, will earn an extra $2,000, while Manager B will take home the extra $10,000 she saved in expenses. In addition, Manager A will get the added personal profit (the bonus) in the first year only (the new operating costs become his baseline in following years). Manager B, on the other hand, will appreciate the $10,000 profit every year to follow as part of her personal take. Imagine if Manager A gets no bonus for cutting costs—he would have no incentive to spend 10 hours of his time trying to save the company $10,000 a year.

Put simply, owners have more of a stake in a business than employees. In company-owned stores, managers are just employees after all. In a franchise, on the other hand, the manager is often the owner and will have a much greater interest in cutting costs, increasing sales, and seeing the business succeed and turn a profit.

Attract Better Management Talent

Why can a franchiser attract better management talent than ordinary corporations? Quite simply, because franchising requires a large financial investment on the part of the franchisee.

Investing in a franchise can cost hundreds of thousands of dollars. Most people able to finance such an investment will be responsible, hard-working, and have business savvy. Additionally, anyone who makes that kind of investment will have more of an incentive to see the investment pay off.

In addition, while corporate positions typically have flat salaries, franchise managers see profit based upon their own hard work and efforts. This is more appealing to managers with expertise and know-how because they are aware of their work ethic and ability to get results.

More Rapid Growth

A lack of capital will decrease growth and an excess of capital will allow more rapid expansion. In the franchise system, capital comes from individual franchisees rather than from the parent company. The franchise system is unique in that, during times of growth the franchiser will see more capital arriving from royalty payments and franchise fees, while the cost of setting up new units is borne mostly by franchisees. As you can imagine, the advantages to the franchiser are enormous. This is the primary reason why franchising system was developed in the first place.

If your company is relatively new, it might be more difficult for you to secure funding for expansion from a bank or other source. Without an extensive track record, banks will be hesitant to loan you large sums of money, even assuming that the market for your product is good. Franchising is a great solution to this problem as the money needed for expansion is supplied by franchisees. Franchisees are usually more willing to invest in a new company — they have the time and incentive to do the extensive research needed to determine whether the business is bound for success or failure. Banks do a more cursory examination when they determine investment risk.

DISADVANTAGES

There are four major disadvantages to franchising. They are as follows:

1. Your goals as a franchiser might differ from the goals of your franchisees.

2. Large franchise systems resist change.

3. Your returns as a franchiser will tend to be lower than if you owned all the units directly.

4. You will see higher costs of doing business.

These are discussed in more detail in the following sections.

Different Goals

While the primary goal of a franchisee is to realize maximum profit (which will increase personal earnings), franchisers are more interested in increasing sales, which will increase their revenue because of higher royalty payments. These goals involve different sales strategies. Franchisees will be looking for business that will decrease costs and time, while franchisers will want more business at every turn.

Coupon promotions started by the franchiser illustrate this conflict well. Coupons that offer products for free or at reduced prices draw in customers. While the franchiser will benefit from this because more products are being sold, increasing royalty payments, the franchisee won't see profit from free or reduced-price products, which will decrease their bottom line.

In addition, conflict often arises during expansions. Franchisers want new stores to open because they receive large franchise fees and more royalty payments. Franchisees, on the other hand, see additional properties close by as threats—new stores can draw customers away from their own stores.

While it is in the franchiser's best interest to keep franchisees happy and franchised units doing well, there is always a give and take between franchiser and franchisee. This can considerably complicate the running of your business.

Resistance to Change

A franchise system is comprised of dozens or even hundreds of owners with individual agendas and goals. As you can imagine, trying to introduce change into the system can be difficult. The franchiser wants to avoid coercion at all costs, so trying to win mass approval for a change is not an easy task. In addition, the franchiser must be aware of legal issues preventing the preferential treatment of one franchisee over another. While regular corporations can change processes or products at one or more stores for experimental purposes, the franchiser cannot make such changes without consent from the franchisee. Any change, to be implemented, must be negotiated and renegotiated with each and every contracted franchisee. This can result in high costs for even very small changes.

Another thing to consider is that as a franchiser, you may not be in touch with the market trends that trigger changes necessary to keep up with changing times. Most change in corporations is in response to shifts in the market or consumer trends; these corporations actively collect data to spot such shifts. In the franchise model, this data would have to be collected from franchisees. Collecting such data would be expensive, time-consuming, and not directly profitable to the franchisee. As a result, the franchiser can expect poor analyses, if any.

Because of the high unit-level costs of introducing new products and services, franchisees are often reluctant to sell new products until the products have a proven track record. Franchises have to spend time and money in training, signage, promotion, and inventory to introduce a new product. They will be unwilling to do so if they are not confident that the product will eventually be a success.

Lower Returns

In setting up a franchise system you will be faced with a number of high costs. The first such cost is setting up the system itself. Because of the necessary legal and financial advice, the cost of training materials, brochures, and UFOCs, and the cost of startup resources for each potential franchise, setting up the system can easily cost hundreds of thousands of dollars.

Also, while the capital necessary to expand your business will be lower, profits generated at the unit level will revert to the franchisee. Research suggests that on average, the franchiser can expect to see $1 per every $3 of profit at the unit level. The other $2 goes into the pocket of the franchisee. In addition, technological changes that will improve efficiency at the unit level will tend to benefit the franchisee and not the franchiser. The only thing that will benefit the franchiser is increased sales (because they result in higher royalties).

Higher Costs of Doing Business

There are several costs associated with the franchise model that are an inherent part of the model and cannot be avoided. These costs are due to the nature of the relationship of franchise units to one another.

First, there is the "free rider" problem. This is a known economic scenario in which the costs of a negative action by one unit are borne by all units, and the cost of a positive action is borne by one member but benefits all members. For example, if one unit of a well-known franchise is sued for discrimination, the negative publicity generated by that unit's actions will tend to reduce sales across the same system. On the other hand, if one unit of a well-known franchise pays for a large billboard advertisement, other units in the area benefit from the advertisement without paying a dime in advertising fees. Such a free rider situation can have profound effects on all units and can add costs otherwise unexpected at the unit level. It can also lead to hostility between unit owners.

The free rider phenomenon can be partly overcome if the franchiser imposes quality and service requirements on the franchisees. Creating a list of approved vendors also helps. These actions also incur costs to the franchiser.

Another example of the higher costs of doing business involves protecting confidential information. Reflect on your business for a moment: do you have any trade secrets, secret recipes, or intellectual property that must be protected from common knowledge for your business to succeed? If so, you will have to pay substantially to protect these secrets. You will have to entrust some amount of knowledge to your franchisees, but for full protection you will need to employ the aid of professionals who can set up elaborate ways to protect your information. You will need to hire legal professionals to create nondisclosure agreements and the like. Costs for these protections are particularly galling because there is no guarantee that your efforts will protect confidential information, and yet, they are necessary costs.

CHAPTER

Franchising Your Business

I f you decide to franchise your business, you must begin thinking about some unique factors. In addition to providing goods and services and keeping accurate financial records, you need to begin directing your energy toward building and managing a franchisee base. Remember that in the eyes of the consumer, there is no difference between you and your franchisees. If you want your business to be reputable, trustworthy, and profitable, you will need to put a great deal of thought into how you select and monitor your franchisees. Remember: they will make or break your business. Also, you need to be able to make sure your business is right for franchising. This chapter will get you started.

LEAP OF FAITH, FROM SMALL BUSINESS TO FRANCHISER: READY, SET, GO!

Can your product or service make it as a franchised offering? Are you worried about competition? Remember: large, established companies, once they feel secure, may stop innovating, promoting, and improving. This leaves room for smaller companies to move in and do it better.

You are ready to franchise if you have done the following.

- Have you developed your prototype operation?

- Do you have an established history of operating success?

- Do you have the team in place set to operate your company as a franchiser?

- Do you have a tactical plan in place for the company as a whole?

- Have you hired people to write, design, print, and otherwise produce all the informational material you will need?

- Do you have enough money?

- Is your UFOC ready to go? What about other essential documents? A UFOC is a legal requirement in many states and must be prepared in a specific fashion. In some states you must also get approval for the UFOC and license your franchise. Check with your local chamber of commerce for rules you will need to follow.

- Are you committed? You must be committed to success and a long-term relationship with your company and its franchisees. It is not just your own prosperity on the line anymore.

You are probably not ready to franchise if you answer "no" to one or more of the following:

- Is my business more than a concept?

- Does my business have a substantial operating history?

- Is my business profitable?

- Is my business experiencing good returns?

- Is my business capable of duplication?

- Can my business system be taught and understood within a reasonable amount of time?

You should also consider the following factors before franchising. Answering these questions will enable you to determine whether your company will be successful as a franchise.

- Are my products and services reputable?

- Are my products and services better than those offered by my competitors?

- Will there be demand for my products and services in my chosen markets?

- Do I have the repeat customers essential for a successfully franchised business?

- Do my goods and services have staying power? (Will there still be a demand for my goods and services at a later time?)

- Can I expect recent or developing trends or legal actions to affect the profitability of my business?

- Can I adjust to market changes such as price adjustments?

- Will my company be able to beat the competition? Will I be able to update my products and services to meet new demands and respond to moves by my competition?

- Is expansion realistic for my company?

You should also answer the following questions to ensure that you are capable of heading a franchiser corporation.

- Do I have the know-how and energy to run my original business while developing a franchise system?

- Do I have the money needed to hire professionals to help me with this endeavor?

- Can I meet the challenges of having units operating in multiple markets?

- Will I be able to find enough qualified franchisees?

- What kind of support will I be able to offer to franchisees, and is it enough?

MY FEE STRUCTURE CAN MAKE OR BREAK ME

When calculating your fee structure, you want to be sure that you do not charge such excessive fees that your franchisees cannot function and thrive. Remember, you will be setting a franchise fee and a royalty rate, and you may be selling goods or leasing property to your franchisees, and also charging them for training expenses. These fees add up. Don't break your franchisees' backs before they hit the ground.

You should consider the following when determining a fee schedule. First, how much do you expect a new franchisee to invest, and how can payments be made? Second, do you usually experience seasonal cash flow problems? If so, adjust the fee schedule to anticipate these problems. Third, what inventory levels do you expect the franchisee will need to maintain, and what is the spoilage rate for food items? Finally, you must earn enough in fees to support your own business. These and other factors must be taken into account.

It is a mistake to look at the fee schedules of your competitors to determine your fee schedule. Your fee schedule should be calculated independently of other companies so that it reflects your company's needs accurately. In the same way, do not try to compete for potential franchisees by pricing your fees competitively with other franchisers. Stay true to your own vision, your own needs, and the health of your company. If you can offer profitability, franchisees will come your way, no matter the fee schedule.

Setting a functional fee schedule is extremely important and should be done with great thought and care. If you need help, you can hire a professional. Professionals with experience setting franchiser fee schedules can be located through the International Association's Council of Franchise Suppliers at **www.franchise. org**.

WHO IS MY IDEAL FRANCHISEE?

While some franchisers will sell a franchise to anyone with a spark of life and the capital, and others select franchisees based upon telephone or mail correspondence, we recommend that you put more effort into your selection. Just as your franchisees should develop a profile of their target consumers for the purposes of choosing a good location, you should develop a profile of the perfect franchisee. You should consider the following factors.

- What kind of person do you need to operate your particular business successfully?

- Will franchisees need a particular level of education or specialty training?

- What do you expect a potential franchisee to bring to the table financially?

- Do you need a franchisee with a particular cultural or sociological awareness?

- Will there be enough suitable franchisees in the markets in which you wish to franchise?

Lure Them In

To attract the right franchisees, you will need something to offer. To understand how to attract owners, learn what the typical franchisee is looking for in a parent company.

WHAT A FRANCHISEE REALLY WANTS

Franchisees choose to invest in a franchise system because they want the benefit of operating a store with a recognizable, reputable brand. In addition, and most importantly, they want to make money. They are not necessarily looking for a particular industry. Instead, they are looking for a profitable business, no matter the product or service offered.

First, you must be able to offer your franchisees a well-planned, operational system that works. You need to have demonstrated some success as a company-owned business before you become a franchiser who is attractive to potential franchisees. To highlight your past success, you should offer informational materials; a thorough description of your business and its operations; training opportunities; a support system; some help in advertising, promotions, and purchasing; and an established, recognizable brand name.

Tell Them How Sweet It Is!

By far, the thing that will be most attractive to franchisees is the potential for great profit. Let your franchisees know that they will make money by investing in your business. However, abide by the law and provide the financial data to back up your claims. It is not necessary to provide an earnings claim, but if the numbers are in your favor, this will make your business more attractive to potential franchisees.

You might want to invest in the development of a sales force specially trained to recruit franchisees. The sales force should be well motivated and should know all there is to know about your business and the industry. They should be well stocked with pamphlets, earnings claims, and other material that highlights the profitability and success of your business. To compensate your sales force, grant them incentives. Make sure they are not rewarded for recruiting unsuitable franchisees. Only reward them when they recruit franchisees with true potential.

Separating the Wheat From the Chaff

Recruiting potential franchisees is only the beginning. One of your most difficult and important tasks will be selecting the ones you want to sell a franchise to. You want to find people who match the profile you designed earlier.

Not as Easy as It Sounds

Remember that hiring and firing at a company-owned business is not the same as managing franchisees. If you think that finding franchisees will be easy because of the skills you developed during years of managing a staff, think again. This is a whole different ball game. Any franchisee to whom you sell will hold a long-term contract. Getting rid of the bad apples will not be easy. You should select your franchisees with much more care than you might have selected regular employees.

You can advertise for franchisees in a number of different media outlets. Attend franchise shows, place ads in newspapers, magazines, and trade publications, use the Internet and the radio, use direct mail, or get "advertorials" placed in business magazines and other suitable publications. Your options for finding potential franchisees are endless. Use your creativity.

HOW DO I NARROW THE FIELD?

As you begin to narrow the field, look at the amount of experience a potential franchisee has in the industry. While experience is not necessary, it surely helps. Particularly if your industry requires some amount of expertise, prior industry-specific experience is something you will really must consider. Experience will most likely be more important than education. Remember, however, that past entrepreneurs are often more difficult to train—they are used to doing things their own way.

You must also consider the potential franchisee's net worth.

Most companies multiply the initial cost of setting up previous company-owned units by four, and require franchisees to be at worth at least that much. The franchisee must be able to make a large initial investment and still have room to breathe until profits start to come in. Franchisees without enough capital struggle and often fail.

You might want to hire a psychological testing company to analyze the psychological profiles of potential franchisees. In this way you can select people with the right levels of determination, cheerfulness, reliability, and other important traits.

I HAVE SOME NEW FRANCHISEES ...NOW WHAT?

First, you must learn or perfect the skills necessary to maintain a successful business relationship, even in the face of conflict.

Keeping Friction to a Minimum

Every franchise you sell will operate as a legally separate and independent entity, yet you must stay on top of all units to maximize the financial potential for everyone. This means that you need to create market saturation and keep your business expanding (so you will make money), while also being sure to limit competition and cannibalism among franchisees (so that they will make money). By carefully placing new stores and limiting the amount of collective action you demand from your franchisees you can avoid making them angry.

Money Keeps Them Happy

If you keep the money rolling in, you will have happy franchisees. To increase cash flow, you should maintain strict quality controls, do market research to create new products and services that will attract new and better customers and thus build recognition for your brand.

Can We Talk?

Be sure to keep in touch with your franchisees. Encourage frequent and productive two-way communication between yourself (or your representatives) and all your franchisees. Communication leads to trust, reliability, and confidence and can alert you to problems and successes your franchisees are experiencing. Successes should be rewarded and problems addressed.

Having a good relationship with your franchisees will also make it easier to introduce new and controversial goods or procedures. If your franchisees feel that they have an open line of communication, they will be less wary of new ideas and will feel like their feedback is important and valuable.

Keeping Tabs

You must be sure to monitor your franchisees. One of the earmarks of a franchise system is consistency and reliability; customers ought to know what to expect when they walk into any of your franchised units. You should provide new franchisees with clear instructions and should be available at all times to answer questions. You should make sure that all instructions and standards are followed and met the same way in every unit.

You can use field audits to gauge compliance. If a unit is not up to standard, you need to take action so that it becomes so. Remind the unit owner of his or her franchise agreement. Your field personnel will prove to be an important part of your support structure. They should be chosen and trained with care and armed with a thorough knowledge of your business, the industry, and how units should be operated. They should be evaluated based on criteria that will measure their ability to get results from the franchisees. Field visits should occur on a set schedule, but the schedule should be modified to meet the needs of problem units. The purpose of field visits is to provide you, the franchiser, with feedback on the operation of each unit, and so these visits benefit the franchise system as a whole.

Inform your franchisees of the need for and purpose behind field visits. The visits should be structured and enhanced as needed to ensure that you get the most out of your efforts. You should work with your field staff and your franchisees in order to foster a feeling of cooperation and helpfulness. Doing so will greatly increase your productivity and the success of your franchisees.

GOING TO MARKET: SMART EXPANSION

Armed with a developed franchise plan and promising potential franchisees, it is time to target the best markets for your business. Do not expand haphazardly. Know your markets and you can identify the right location for expansion. You should have a primary and secondary market in mind. You should also have a plan in place for expansion timing and an idea of the critical mass for your market. Focus your plan so that your expansion is proactive rather than reactive.

Demographics, manageability, and customer access are important factors when choosing locations for units. Remember that most of the management of the unit will fall into the franchisee's hands, but also that units must be placed to minimize the cost of field visits and to avoid cannibalism while allowing market saturation. You can help your franchisees find suitable locations, or you can simply approve chosen locations. Alternatively, you can choose to play no role in location selection. We highly recommend that you study locations for suitability.

WAVE OF THE FUTURE: TACTICAL EXECUTION

You should try to develop a tactical strategy for managing your business. This means that those people who come up with tactics should also execute those tactics. This is the way that most successful, modern businesses operate today. You should strive to create a centralized management based at headquarters, from which you dole out the strategizing for various aspects of your business to the parties with the expertise and knowledge to make the best decision.

Each member of the organization should be involved in its improvement and should be thinking about ways to make things better. The members of your organization should be committed to the success of the company and have a clear understanding of its vision. Emphasis should be placed on learning, experimentation, and adaptation. Successes should be celebrated by all. Flexibility should be part of your management strategies, and results should be measured and evaluated quickly so that improvements can be made as soon as possible.

CORPORATE CULTURE: THE TIES THAT BIND

Developing a pervasive corporate culture for your company will help maintain consistency, reliability, and quality throughout the organization, while also increasing the effect of branding. Members of the organization with a clear understanding of the corporate culture conduct themselves and make decisions in accordance with the image you wish to present. Corporate culture gives everyone a direction and purpose. It is undeniably important for franchise systems to have a defined corporate culture.

KNOWLEDGE IS POWER

A key to running your franchised company smoothly will be your ability to gather and disseminate important information quickly to all members of your organization. This information can be either anecdotal or data-based. In either case, letting all members of the organization know what is going on within the company will cut back on problems and lead to better decisions.

You should be aware of the practices of your competitors at all times. You should also be conducting constant research into the needs and desires of your customer base. Consistently gather feedback from all your franchisees as well as from your field agents and headquarters staff. Also, remain in communication with your vendors; they will provide you with useful information.

LIKE IT OR NOT, YOU NEED AN ATTORNEY

Franchising has many legal implications. Don't skimp. Hire a legal professional to help you with the paperwork. Your UFOC, legal agreements, and other documents need to be prepared according to the law. You will be well served by creating a "business overlay." This is a condensed version of your tactical plan that will give your lawyer a clear understanding of where your business is heading. From this document the attorney should be able to create a UFOC and other legal documents.

Be sure that the completed documents are in line with your plan of business. If you find something odd, discuss it with your attorney who is there to serve you.

SELF-SERVICE NOT RECOMMENDED

Various prepackaged franchising kits are available, featuring fill-in-the-blank forms and cut-and-paste attempts to help you create your own legal documents from a common template. These kits are inexpensive when compared to hiring an attorney, but they are also ineffective and dangerous. Creating a franchise is complex and cannot be boiled down to a cut-and-paste template. If you are willing to cut corners in this area, perhaps you should think twice about franchising.

BEWARE THE "FRANCHISE PACKAGERS"

While you should hire an attorney with experience in franchise law, you want to avoid "franchise packagers." These individuals who act as brokers will offer to sell franchises on your behalf. They often use questionable legal materials, and try to cram your company into a marketing mold they also use for companies dissimilar to yours.

To find the best professionals, talk to other people in your industry or to other franchisers. Make sure you meet with and interview a number of candidates before making your choice. You want to find someone with experience both in franchising and in your industry and whose fees you can afford — there is nothing wrong with asking to see a fee schedule. After you find a good prospect, get in touch with that person's clients, and ask about results.

When choosing an attorney, make sure you feel comfortable sharing personal and financial information. Check the American Bar Association Franchising Forum at **www.abanet.org.** Also check with the International Association's Council of Franchise Suppliers for good referrals.

LOOK OUT WORLD, HERE I COME: GLOBAL EXPANSION

Do not assume you can succeed internationally because you have succeeded in the domestic market. While global expansion can give you added prestige, increase pervasive branding, and significantly widen your customer base, international markets differ greatly from those in the United States. You must time your expansion wisely, have the right reasons for it, and choose partners who will help you to expand smoothly.

Some things to consider before a global expansion are (1) the economy of the area into which you want to expand, (2) the stability of the government and possible corruption, (3) means of supplying overseas franchises in that area, (4) legal and cultural factors, and (5) the likelihood of finding qualified franchisees to run the units overseas.

Money, Money, Money

You should also take financial considerations into account, and we are not talking about your own. There is widespread international poverty, and many local populations have less money to spend on your goods or services. It could take longer than expected to realize profit from international units. In addition, expectations about wages and benefits will differ, and you should be prepared to meet or exceed the standards in any country.

When it comes to considering your own financial situation, you should know that studies suggest that up to 80 percent of franchise fees are returned to the unit in servicing costs and other expenses associated with running a unit overseas. Just sending a field agent to check out and offer help to overseas units can put a dent in franchise fees.

Yes, You Need Another Attorney

You will need to hire an attorney with experience in international franchise law, because each country has its own laws governing franchising. This attorney should be able to advise you on expansion moves and steer you away from legal pitfalls you might otherwise encounter. For example, the attorney should be able to create a UFOC that is in compliance with a country's laws. Do not forget potential differences in lease terms, labor laws, tariffs, prohibitions on import, and trademark laws. In addition, a consultation with your attorney before taking on each new franchisee is a good idea, especially if the attorney has connections in that location.

There are a number of resources for finding a good international franchise attorney. First, check the International Franchise Association's Council of Franchise Suppliers (**www.franchise. org**). You can also check with the American Bar Association's Franchise Forum (**www.abanet.org**) or with the International Bar Association's Section of Business Law International Franchise Committee in London (phone number 44 171 629 1206 or at **www. ibanet.org**). Finally, you could contact Law Business Research Ltd., also in London, at 44 171 486 2611.

Striking the International Deal

In addition to presenting each potential foreign franchisee with an updated UFOC, you will need to ensure that the franchisee understands your business and corporate culture. Similarity in language does not mean similarity in thought, so don't assume that because the potential franchisee speaks and understands English he is approaching your business from the same cultural perspective. His notions of customer relations, marketing, and other aspects of your business could differ significantly due to his own cultural assumptions. Before taking on a foreign franchisee, you must be sure that your franchisee sees the same big picture as you, in terms of your business

There are many other issues that you will need to address when expanding globally.

- What are typical hours of operation for the country?

- Similarly, when does the weekend fall?

- What menu or cultural restrictions might you face?

- Will you need to invoice or receive royalties differently?

- Are there monetary exchange rules in place that will make converting your fees and other royalties into U.S. currency a problem?

You can get some idea of what to expect from various nations by checking the Web site of Piper Rudnick, Gray and Carry, Washington, D.C., at **www.piperrudnick.com**.

How Do I Know When to Expand Overseas?

You may be ready to expand internationally if you have an extremely profitable and solid domestic business and have put some intensive planning into a long-term commitment to overseas expansion. You need to be willing to transfer resources and manpower to overseas developments, away from domestic establishments. Overconfidence, a large ego, unsolicited invitations from overseas markets, and schemes for fixing cash flow problems are not good reasons for international expansion.

You should not pursue global expansion if your management is not willing or able to commit to the long-term; if your product doesn't fit the standards of the areas into which you want to expand; if your business will not be able to adapt to local standards and customs; or if the area you want to expand into has governmental or societal instability.

Who Will Be My Partners in This Faraway Land?

We have already mentioned the cultural barriers you might encounter in locating qualified foreign franchisees. Your choice of organization structure can significantly cut down on such problems: consider master franchising, area development, or a joint venture. The first will enable you to take advantage of the franchisee's cultural knowledge, while the second and third will give you, as the franchiser, an increased amount of control over the franchisee's actions.

Cultural differences aside, there are other problems you will be sure to encounter at some point in working with foreigners. Foreign nations often have less capital for business ventures, so finding a franchisee with enough money to purchase and keep the franchise afloat can be quite difficult. You will also need to locate franchisees with the level of attentiveness, dedication, and motivation you are used to encountering in American businesspeople. Most importantly, you will need to find franchisees with whom you can entrust the reputation of your business. You will be introducing your company to new markets, and you must be able to trust your franchisees to make decisions and operate their franchises in ways that will earn your company international respect and a continuing good reputation.

Screen all candidates carefully. You can check in the following places for this kind of information:

- National franchise associations;

- Franchise attorneys serving the local area;

- If possible, the local office associated with your domestic accounting firm;

- Interpol;

- The U.S. Embassy or Consulate in the location;

- International credit and reference services;

- The International Trade Administration's Trade Information Center (800-UDA-TRADE).

Where Do I Begin My Search?

The following resources are some great places to begin your search for qualified and trustworthy potential foreign franchisees.

- Attend one of the Certified Trade Missions sponsored by the U.S. Department of Commerce and the IFA. Usually, three 10- to 12-day missions are sponsored annually. You can meet face-to-face with potential franchisees during these trips. For more information, see **www.ita.doc.gov**.

- Attend the International Franchise Exposition (201-226-1130; **www.franchiseexpo.com**).

- Check with local industry associations, embassies, or chambers of commerce.

- Check with national franchise associations.

- Check with the World Franchise Council (see **www.fca.com.au**).

- Obtain referrals from local consultants and attorneys.

How Do I Negotiate an International Deal?

Understanding and trust are primary. You should review your rights, your potential franchisee's rights, and all terms and conditions before selling a unit. You should literally go over everything to clear up all misunderstandings and be sure that language or cultural differences are not interfering with understanding one another. In some cultures you must establish a friendship before establishing a business relationship.

You should be willing to be somewhat flexible when negotiating, but don't be overly accommodating. You shouldn't be so flexible that you recruit someone without the requisite capital and expertise to run the franchise. If the potential franchisee is unhappy with your fee schedule, do not simply lower fees. Rather, offer more in return for the same fee; for example, more training, support, materials, advertising, and even, perhaps, discounts.

IMPORTING A FOREIGN FRANCHISE TO U.S. SOIL

Franchising is not only an American phenomenon, and there are many foreign franchise companies that would love to set roots in American soil. Potential exists for these organizations given the extensive availability of American capital.

Many of the same factors should be considered for importing a franchise into the United States as for exporting one out. The following issues should be addressed:

- Do you have a successful domestic business that will be able to support an expansion?

- Have you previously expanded successfully outside your home nation?

- Have you done sufficient research to determine the best U.S. market into which to expand? There are extraordinarily different markets, all within the borders of the United States.

- What kind of local support will you be able to offer? Will you establish field offices?

- Will you be offer training material in both English and Spanish?

- Is there a U.S. demand for your products or services?

What Challenges Will Foreign Franchiser Likely Face In the United States?

First, you will need to think about the adaptability of your products or services. Will you be able to adapt your product to the needs of American consumers, and if so, how? Second, will you be able to find American suppliers, or will you need to spend significant time and money importing your supplies? Also, will your brand be able to compete with the large number of reputable brands in the United States?

If your expansion fails, for whatever reason, do you have exit strategies? How will you resolve any disputes?

Finally, will your American employees feel welcome within your corporate culture? Will language be a problem? Will your American employees have trouble communicating with central management office overseas?

Never forget: the U.S. market is vast and largely unforgiving. The excessive amount of established competition makes it difficult for any new, foreign presence to get a foothold and succeed. You must be able to provide the same level of standards as U.S. companies, and you must be able to offer a UFOC.

CHAPTER 18

Franchising and the Law

Franchise systems are legally regulated. If you are thinking of franchising your business, you must be aware of the various legal obligations by which you, as a franchiser, will need to abide. In this chapter we will outline some important legal issues. Franchise regulations will be discussed according to both state and federal laws, and some pros and cons of operating within various state frameworks will be analyzed.

FEDERAL LAW

As mentioned earlier, franchisers are required by the Federal Trade Commission to provide certain information to prospective franchisees, including details of the history, operations and governing principles of the company. This information is contained in the UFOC and must be provided at least 10 days in advance of any signing. However, franchisers selling to overseas franchisees or to franchisees meeting the criteria of "sophistication" do not need to provide this document. The FTC has created a standard

UFOC template, which it provides to franchisers. Table 18.1 lists items required for disclosure in a UFOC document; a more detailed discussion of the UFOC can be found in chapter 3.

INSERT TABLE 18.1:
ITEMS REQUIRED FOR DISCLOSURE IN A UFOC

1.	The franchiser and predecessors
2.	Business experience of persons affiliated with the franchiser
3.	Litigation history
4.	Bankruptcy history
5.	Initial fee
6.	Other fees
7.	Initial investment
8.	Restrictions of franchisee sourcing
9.	Franchisee's obligations
10.	Financing
11.	Franchiser's obligations
12.	Territory
13.	Trademarks and service marks
14.	Patents and copyrights
15.	Obligation of the franchisee to participate in the business
16.	Restrictions on franchisee sale of goods and services
17.	Renewal and termination
18.	Arrangements with public figures
19.	Earnings claims
20.	Statistics on system
21.	Audited financial statements

22.	Contracts
23.	Acknowledgment of receipt

Compliance with the UFOC requires an audited financial statement, driving up franchise expenses significantly because of hiring both the auditing firm and an experienced franchise attorney. Furthermore, if you make claims about franchisee earnings from your outlets, you need to provide additional disclosure about those earnings.

STATE LAW

State laws often govern two key aspects of franchising. First, state regulations may dictate what can and cannot be done by franchisers to sell franchises and may include restrictions concerning registration of the company and the provision of information to potential franchisees. Second, state laws may govern the relationship between franchisers and franchisees, including issues such as the termination of a franchise agreement.

Not every state has franchise laws; some states have only laws governing the first aspect of franchising and some only the second. There are large differences between franchise laws from state to state. Consult a legal professional about state laws. It is important to be acquainted with your own state's laws as well as the laws of the states in which you have operating franchises.

REGISTRATION STATES

In states requiring the registration of franchised companies, franchisers must furnish state regulatory agencies with a UFOC before starting any franchising activity. In most states you can provide the same version as you gave the FTC; California, Indiana, Maryland, Minnesota, Rhode Island, South Dakota, Virginia, and the District of Columbia require different versions. Registration states also require you to file annual, sometimes quarterly, reports containing specific information. Recently, registration has been simplified by an electronic registration system that allows franchisers to register with all registration states simultaneously.

Why do states require registration? First, the theory is that if they are required to register, franchisers will be more likely to provide accurate information to franchisees. Second, franchisees are afforded some level of protection through the registration process: fees might be required to be put into an escrow account; bonds could be issued protecting franchisees from an undercapitalization of the franchiser; and any performance claims made by the franchiser to attract potential franchisees can be more easily verified.

As a franchiser, you must document any changes made to your franchise system, and you must provide updated versions of your UFOC to registration states. Things that must be documented include changes to your fee schedule, franchisee obligations, or the legal structure of the company; updated financial information; or any programs added or modified concerning your interaction with franchisees. It is in your interest to minimize negotiations with franchisees and to offer standardized agreements to all franchisees to avoid refiling the UFOC frequently.

Because of the large regulatory burden, you might decide to avoid operating in registration states altogether, as do almost 50 percent of existing franchised organizations. By operating in registration states, however, you receive a number of benefits. Some estimates show that the oversight system provided by registration states has made companies operating in registration states 22 percent more successful on average. Also, franchisee confidence is bolstered by your willingness to comply with state regulations; they take it as a sign you are on the up-and-up. Finally, the larger your company, the cheaper it is to operate in registration states; conversely, the larger your company, the more expensive operating outside of registration states becomes.

RELATIONSHIP STATES

Relationship laws are typically put into place to protect franchisees. The laws make sure, for example, that franchisers provide an acceptable reason for contract breaches such as termination. Relationship laws give franchisees a way to fight any contract breaches by the franchiser. However, such protections also raise franchiser costs, causing many of them to demand higher royalty payments from units located within relationship states.

Franchisees will be more willing to take on a unit with your franchise if you operate in relationship states. Relationship laws simply make franchisees more comfortable in their investment. At the same time, relationship laws make getting rid of ineffective or problem franchisees difficult. Table 18.2 lists states with different relationship provisions.

INSERT TABLE 18.2:

STATES WITH DIFFERENT RELATIONSHIP PROVISIONS

States That Require Cause for Termination	States That Allow Cure in Termination
Arkansas	Arkansas
California	California
Connecticut	Hawaii
Delaware	Illinois
Hawaii	Michigan
Illinois	Minnesota
Indiana	Washington
Michigan	Wisconsin
Minnesota	
Nebraska	
New Jersey	
Virginia	
Washington	
Wisconsin	

FRANCHISER CERTIFICATION

Getting your franchise certified will win you respect and trust from potential franchisees. Through winning contests or being ranked by media outlets, you will gain recognition and much-desired notice. Recognition by any reputable medium, be it a magazine, newspaper, or some other organization, will benefit your company more than you can imagine.

You should apply for membership in important trade associations such as the International Franchise Association. Membership is not a given: only about 600 of 2,500 existing franchises are members. To be a member, you must be able to demonstrate higher than normal standards, that you have no legal violations on record, and that you operate in compliance with all state and federal regulations. Membership is a sign of quality, reliability, and profitability.

CHAPTER 19

Franchising Resources

COMPANIES OFFERING FRANCHISING

This is a partial, random listing of companies who offer franchising. They are listed in alphabetical order. Listing includes the company name, a contact title, contact name, address, city, state, ZIP, phone number, extension, second phone number (if available), fax, e-mail, Web site and type of franchise.

AIM Mail Centers
Amailcenter Franchise
Corporation
postal and business service
Steve Sawitz , Franchise
Development
15550 Rockfield Blvd, Suite D
Irvine, CA 92618
PH: (949) 837-4151
Fax: (949) 837-4537
franchiseinfo@
aimmailcenters.com
www.aimmailcenters.com

Aire Serv Heating & Air
Conditioning
Aire Serv Corporation
the nation's only franchise
opportunity focused on heating,
ventilation, and air conditioning
maintenance and repair services.
Aire Serv's primary client base
includes residential and light
commercial applications.
Doyle James, President
1020 N University Parks Dr.
Waco, TX 76707-3858

PH: (800) 583-2662
Fax: (800) 378-9480
DwyerGroup.com
www.discoversas.com

Alternative Board The
*peer advisory boards and coaching
services*
1640 Grant Street, Suite 200
Denver, CO 80203
PH: (303) 839-1200
Toll-free: (800) 727-0126
Fax: (303) 839-0012
salesinfo@tabboards.com
www.tabboards.com

AmericInn International Inc.
Jon Kennedy, Senior Vice
President
250 Lake Dr E
Chanhassen, MN 55317-9364
PH: (952) 294-5000
Fax: (952) 294-5001
franchise@americinn.com,
www.americinn.com

**American Asphalt
Sealcoating Franchise Corp.**
asphalt maintenance
Todd Tornstrom, CEO
PO BOX 600
Chesterland, OH 44026
PH: (440) 729-8080
Toll-free: (888) 603-7325
Fax: (440) 729-2231

asphaltusa@aol.com
www.aasfc.com

American Lenders Service Co.
collateral recovery and auction
Jim Golden, President
PO Box 7238
Odessa, TX 79760-7238
PH: (432) 332-0361
Fax: (432) 335-1065
www.americanlenders.com

Americandy USA Candy Inc.
Omar Tatum, President/
Founder
3618 Saint Germaine Ct
Louisville, KY 40207
PH: (502) 583-1776
Fax: (502) 583-1776,
americandy@aol.com
www.americandybar.com

**Amron School of the Fine
Arts John & Joe Fashions Inc.**
Norma Williams, President
1315 Medlin Rd
Monroe, NC 28112
(704) 283-4290

Andy Oncall Franchising, Inc.
a handyman repair service
company that sends a qualified
craftsman for a FREE Estimate to
homeowners needing small jobs,
repairs and maintenance.
Franchise Dept
921 E Main St
Chattanooga, TN 37408-1524
Toll-Free: (877) 263-9662
Fax: (423) 622-0580
Info@andyoncall.com
www.andyoncall.com

Animal Adventure Inc.
retail pet store
Mike Edwards, President
5453 S 76th St
Greendale, WI 53129-1130
PH: (800) 289-5665
Fax: (414) 423-7351
mike@animaladventurepets.
com
www.animaladventurepets.com

Anne Penman Laser Therapy
stop smoking, weight reduction
and stress relief services
Franchise Department
6690 Roswell RD NE, Suite 350
Atlanta, GA 30328
PH: (404) 256-2609
Fax: (404) 256-2234
www.annepenmanlaser
therapy.com

Arctic Circle Restaurants Inc.
George D. Morgan, Executive
Vice President
411 W 7200 S, Suite 200
Midvale, UT 84047-0339
PH: (801) 561-3620
Fax: (801) 561-9646

Arthur Rutenberg Homes Inc.
home building
Raja Jaghab, Senior Vice
President
13922 58th St N
Clearwater, FL 33760-3771
PH: (727) 536-5900
Fax: (727) 538-9089
rjaghab@arhomes.com
www.arhomes.com

Atlantic Mover Parts &
Supples Inc.
Robert J. Bettelli, President
13421 SW 14th Pl
Davie, FL 33325
PH: (954) 474-4942,
Fax: (954) 475-0414
ampsone@bellsouth.net

Arthur Murray Dance Studios
Tony K Cadianl, First Vice
President
1077 Ponce de Leon Blvd
Coral Gables, FL 33134
PH: (305) 445-9645
Fax: (305) 445-0451
www.arthurmurray.com

Babies 'N' Bells Inc.
Dara Craft, CEO
4489 Mira Vista Dr
Frisco, TX 75034-7519
Toll-Free: (888) 418-2229
Fax: (972) 335-3535
corp@babiesnbells.com
www.babiesnbells.com

Baby News
children's stores
Roger O'Callaghan, President
6909 Las Positas Rd, Suite A
Livermore, CA 94551-5113
PH: (925) 245-1370
Fax: (925) 245-1376
info@stanforddistributing.com
www.babynewsstores.com

Baja Sol Tortilla Grill
fresh Mexican fast-casual food
Mike Platt
7173 Oak Pointe Curve
Bloomington, MN 55438-3403
PH: (612) 280-1467
Fax: (952) 944-2001

mikeeplatt@aol.com
www.bajasol.com

**Baker Bros American Deli,
BB Franchising Inc.**
Ralph Kinder
5500 Greenville Ave, Suite 1102
Dallas, TX 75206
PH: (214) 696-8780
Fax: (214) 696-8809
www.bkersbrosdeli.com

**Bar-B-Cutie Franchise
Systems**
Brett McFarland
5120 Virginia Way, Suite B-23
Brentwood, TN 37027
PH: (615) 372-0707
Fax: (615) 372-0705
inquiry@bar-b-cutie.com,
www.bar-b-cutie.com

Bath Fitter Franchising Inc.
Joe Fasoli
27 Berard Dr # 2701
South Burlington, VT
   05403-5810
Toll Free: (877) 422-2322
Fax: (450) 472-3504
infobath@bathfitter.com
www.bathfitter.com

Batteries Plus America's Battery Experts, Batteries Plus LLC
Rod Tremelling, Franchise Development Executive
925 Walnut Ridge Dr.
Hartland, WI 53029
PH: (800) 274-9155
Fax: (262) 912-3100
franchishing@batteriesplus.com
www.bateriesplus.com

Bearcom Building Services Inc.
commercial cleaning
Joseph Jenkins
7022 S 400 W
Midvale, UT 84047-1033
PH: (801) 569-9500
Fax: (801) 569-8400
joseph@bearcomservices.com
www.bearcomeservices.com,

Ben & Jerry's Franchising Inc.
ice cream
Theresa Lafountain, Franchise Sales Coordinator
30 Community Dr
South Burlington, VT 05403
PH: (802) 846-1500 ext. 7818
Fax: (802) 846-1538
theresa.lafountain@benjerry.com
www.benjerry.com

Benchmark Group
architecture and engineering firm
Jim Parks, Director of Marketing
121 W Walnut St
Rogers, AZ 72756-6662
PH: (479) 636-5004,
Fax: (479) 636-9687
jim@bgark.com
www.bgark.com

Best Bagels In Town
Jay Squatrigilla, President
480 Patchogue Rd. #19
Holbrook, NY 11741
PH: (631) 472-4104
Fax: (631) 472-4105
jaybbit@optonline.net
www.bestbagelsintown.net

BlackJack Pizza Franchising Inc.
pizza delivery
9088 Marshall Ct
Westminster, CO 80031-2920
PH: (303) 426-1921
Fax: (303) 428-0174
www.blackjackpizza.com

Blinds Shades & Shutters
Al Asano
269 Market Place Blvd #342
Cartersville, GA 30121-2235
PH: (770) 975-1688
Fax: (770) 529-9018
info@clean-money.com
www.clean-money.com

Border Magic
Franchise Department
1503 County Road 2700 N
Rantoul, IL 61866-9705
PH: (217) 892-2954
Fax: (217) 893-3739
www.bordermagic.com

Borvin Beverage Franchise Corp.
Don Mikovch, President
1022 King St
Alexandria, VA 22314
PH: (703) 683-9463
Fax: (703) 836-6654
info@borviabeverage.com
www.borvinbeverage.com

Brake Masters Systems Inc.
automotive repair and service
6179 E Broadway Blvd
Tucson, AZ 85711-4028
PH: (520) 512-0000 ext. 33
Fax: (866) 459-8731
moshei@brakemasters.com
www.brakemasters.com

Bri-Lee Enterprises
car detailing
241 W Grant St
New Castle, PA 16101-2212
PH: (724) 658-2005
Fax: (724) 658-6226

Buck's Pizza
PO BOX 405
Du Bois, PA 15801
PH: (814) 371-3076
Fax: (814) 371-4214,
www.buckspizz.com

BYOB Water Store
retail water and water processing equipment store
Richard L Cure
1288 W Main St, Suite 103
Lewisville, TX 75067
PH: (972) 219-1551

Captain D's Inc.
Seafood QSR
1717 Elm Hill Pike
Nashville, TN 37210-3707
Toll Free: (800) 550-4877
Fax: (615) 231-2734
franchise_info@captainds.com
www.captainds.com

Card One Inc.
secured credit cards
Raymond A Strohl
1097 Irongate Ln, Suite C
Columbus, OH 43213
PH: (614) 864-1440

Carpet Network Inc.
mobile floorcovering and windows
Jennifer Ostroff , Vice
President for Franchise
Development
109 Galther Dr
Mount Laurel, NJ 08054-1749
Toll Free: (800) 428-1067
Fax: (856) 273-0160
franchise@carpetnetwork.com
www.carpetnetwork.com

Casa Mia Restaurants
Robert Knudson, President
716 Plum St SE
Olympia, WA 98501
PH: (360) 352-0440,
www.casamiarestaurants.com

Cats Inn, The
cat boarding
95 S Windsor Ave,
Brightwaters, NY 11718,
PH: (877) 228-7466
Fax: (631) 969-9264
info@catsinn.com

Chicago Tastee-freez Corp.
*Tastee Freez franchise for Illinois
counties of Kane, Cook, Lake and
DuPage*
Ann Rose or Michael Scott
5627 Dempster St
Morton Grove, IL 60053
PH: (773) 334-3300

Fax: (847) 498-2295
mkscott1@excite.com

Chicago's Pizza Franchise
1111 N Broadway St
Greenfield, IN 46140-1212
PH: (317) 467-1877

Child I.D. Program Inc., The
Marc Bakerman, President
705 Lakefield Rd, Building G
Westlake Village, CA 91361
PH: (805) 557-0577
Fax: (805) 557-0587
info@4childid.com,
www.4childid.com

CiCi's Pizza
Cici Enterprises LP
Angie Zimmermann
1080 W Bethel RD
Coppell, TX 75019
PH: (972) 745-4200
Fax: (972) 745-4204
finformation@cicispizza.com
www.cicispizza.com

Closet Factory, The
Sheilah Dwyer, Director of
Franchise Development
12800 S Broadway
Los Angeles, CA 90061
PH: (310) 715-1000
Fax: (310) 324-6019
info@closetfactory.com
www.closetfact.com

Cock of the Walk Keelboat Concepts, Inc.
seafood and steak restaurant
Mike Rickels, Owner/Director
PO Box 2324
Daphne, AL 36526
PH: (251) 626-2322
www.cockofthewalk.biz

Coffee News USA
weekly restaurant publication
William A Buckley, President
120 Linden St
Bangor, ME 04401
PH: (207) 941-0860
Fax: (207) 941-0150
bill@coffeenewsusa.com
www.coffeenewsusa.com,

Coit Services Inc.
Nick Granato
897 Hinckley Rd
Burlingame, CA 94010-1502
PH: (650) 697-5471, 121
Fax: (650) 697-1861
nick.granato@coit.com
www.coit.com

College Prospects of America
*marketing high school students
and athletes to colleges*
Tracy L Jackson
12682 College Prospect Dr
Logan, OH 43138
PH: (410) 385-6624
Toll-free: (888) 275-2762

Fax: (740) 385-9065
homeoffice@cpoa.com
www.cpoa.com

Company Corporation
2711 Centerville Rd, Suite 400
Wilmington, DE, 19808-1645
PH: (302) 636-5440
www.corporate.com

Computer Maintenance Service
Floyd MacKenzie, General
Manager
PO Box 335
San Marcos, TX 78667-0335,
PH: (830) 629-1400

Computertots & Computer Explorers
Jenny Langfeld
12715 Telge Rd
Cypress, TX 77429-2289
Toll Free: (888) 638-8722
Fax: (281) 256-4178
ctsales@iced.net
www.computertots.com

Concerto Networks
business technology services
610 West Ash St, Suite 1501
San Diego, CA 92101-3546
PH: (619) 501-4530
Fax: (619) 501-4531
info@concertonetworks.com
www.concertonetworks.com

Cookie Bouquet/Cookies by Design
David Patterson, CEO
1865 Summit Ave
Plano, TX 75074
PH: (972) 398-9536
Fax: (972) 398-9542
frandevelopment@mgwmall.
com
www.cookiesbydesign.com

Corn Dog Factory International
two quick service restaurants, Corn Dog Factory and Nach-o-Fast
12 S Main St, Suite 206
Layton, UT 84041
PH: (801) 546-9909
Fax: (801) 546-9901
info@corndogfactory.com
www.corndogfactory.com

CottageCare Inc.
residential house cleaning
Brian Nagel
6323 W 110th St
Overland Park, KS 66211-1509
PH: (800) 718-8100
Fax: (913) 469-0822
bnagel@cottagecare.com
www.cottagecare.com

Creative World School Franchising Co Inc.
Duane McCabe
13315 Orange Grove Dr
Tampa, FL 33618
PH: (813) 968-9154
Fax: (813) 264-7266
cworld@tampabay.rr.com
www.creativeworldschool.com

Crown Trophy Inc.
awards and recognition franchise
Scott Kelly, Executive Vice President
9 Skyline Dr
Hawthorne, NY 10532-2100
Toll-Free: (800) 583-8228, ext. 203
Fax: (914) 347-0211
scott@crowntrophy.com
www.crownfranchise.com

Cruise Lines Reservation Center
travel services
Bernard Korn, President
2 Emily Ct
Moriches, NY 11955
PH: (561) 482-9557

CruiseOne
home-based cruise travel agency
Gene Brezenoff
1415 NW 62nd St, Suite 205
Fort Lauderdale, FL 33309
PH: (954) 958-3701
Fax: (954) 958-3697
franchise@cruiseone.com
www.cruiseonefranchise.com

Damon's Grill
casual dining restaurant
Damon's International Inc.
Ed Williams, Vice President of
Development
4645 Executive Dr
Columbus, OH 43220
PH: (614) 442-7900
Fax: (614) 442-7787
franchise@damons.com
www.damons.com

Décor & You Inc
decorating products/services
900 Main St. S, Bldg 2
Southbury, CT 6488
PH: (203) 264-3500
Toll-free: (800) 477-3326
Fax: (203) 264-5095
info@decorandyou.com
www.decorandyou.com

Delta Janitorial Systems Inc.
janitorial services and supplies
Rhona Springfield

2701 W Airport Fwy, Suite 118
Irving, TX 75062-6068
PH: (972) 256-6475
Fax: (972) 256-4194
www.deltajanitorial.com

Denny's
Dory Pjerf, Franchise
Development
203 E Main St
Spartanburg, SC 29319
PH: (800) 304-0222
Fax: (864) 597-7708
www.dennys.com

Dent Doctor
same day auto appearance service
Tom Harris, President
PO BOX 7727
Little Rock, AR 72217
PH: (501) 224-0500
Fax: (501) 224-0507
info@dentdoctor.com
www.dentdoctor.com

Detail Plus Car Appearance Systems
auto detailing
R.L.Abraham, President
PO Box 20755
Portland, OR 97294-0755
PH: (800) 284-0123,
Fax: (503) 251-5975
detailplus@detailplus.com
www.detailplus.com

Discovery Map International
317 Commercial Ave, Ste 100
Anacortes, WA 98221
PH: (360) 588-0144
Fax: (360) 588-8344,
www.discoverymap.com

Diversifoods Inc.
candy, popcorn, and other snacks
Barbara Wellard
14052 W Petronella Dr, Suite 102
Libertyville, IL 60048-9512
PH: (847) 968-4415
Fax: (847) 968-5535
tropikhdqr@aol.com
www.tropiksun.com

Doc Chey's Asian Kitchen
Brad Spratte
1409 N Highland Ave NE
Suite M
Atlanta, GA 30306
PH: (404) 541-1077
Toll Free Fax: (800) 758-9894
franchise@doocheys.com
www.doccheys.com

Dollar Discount Stores of America
Stacey Insel
1362 Naamans Creek Rd
Boothwyn, PA 19061-1618
PH: (610) 497-1991
Fax: (610) 485-6439
info@dollardiscount.com
www.dollardiscount.com

Dollar More Or Less
Ted Tepsich
1061 E. Flamingo Rd. Suite 516
Las Vegas, NV 89119-7448
PH: (702) 737-9228
Fax: (702) 737-9218
123store@dollarmoreorless.com
www.adollarmoreorless.com

Dolphin Publications of America Inc.
Brad Weber, National
Marketing Director
1235 Sunset Grove Rd
Fallbrook, CA 92028-8328
PH: (760) 723-2283
Fax: (760) 728-3145

Drama Kids International Inc.
drama classes for children and teenagers
Margie Macielak, Director of
Franchise Development
32258 Corporate Court
Ellicott City, MD 21042
PH: (410) 480-2015, ext. 30
Fax: (410) 480-2026
margie@dramakids.com
www.dramakids.com

DreamMaker Bath & Kitchen
remodeling
Karen Faudi, V.P. of Franchising
1020 N University Parks Dr
Waco, TX 76707-3858
PH: (800) 253-9153
Fax: (254) 745-2588
franchising@dwyergroup.com
**www.dreammaker-remodel.
com**

Dryclean USA
drycleaning
Dan Biggs, Director of
Operations
290 NE 68th St
Miami, FL 33138
PH: (305) 754-9966
Fax: (305) 754-8010
sales@drycleanusa.com
www.drycleanusa.com

**Dynamic Development
Associates**
leadership development
Bill Eggert, President
381 Bridle Ln
PO Box 18
Media, PA 19063-1930
PH: (610) 565-3860
Fax: (610) 565-5557

Educational Outfitters
school apparel corporate wear
fundraising

Brian Elrod
8002 E Brainerd Rd
Chattanooga, TN 37421
PH: (423) 894-1222
Fax: (423) 894-9222
info@educationaloutfitters.
com
www.educationaloutfitters.com

**Electonic Tax Filers, The
St. Simons Corporation**
Rachel Wishon
PO Box 2077
Cary, NC 27512
PH: (919) 469-0651
Toll-free: (800) 945-9277
Fax: (919) 460-5935
rachelwishon@aol.com
www.electronictaxfilers.com

Elmer's Restaurants Inc.
Jerry Scott, Vice President
11802 SE Stark St
Portland, OR 97216-3762
PH: (503) 252-1485
Fax: (503) 252-6706
www.elmers-restaurants.com

Entrees Dinnerprises
Don Shipe , Founder-Owner
3 Lombardy Terrace
Benbrook, TX 76132
PH: (817) 737-5584
entrees@juno.com
www.entreesdinnerprises.com

EPIC Systems Inc.
janitorial services
Jeffrey Schaper John
402 E Maryland St
Evansville, IN 47711-5110
PH: (812) 428-7750
Fax: (812) 428-4162
jrs@speedex.net

Express Oil Change
automotive services
Heather Barrow, Franchise
Development Associate
190 W Valley Ave
Birmingham, AL 35209
PH: (888) 945-1771, ext. 114
Fax: (205) 940-6025
hbarrow@expressoil.com
www.expressoil.com

Extreme Pizza/OOC Inc.
gourmet pizza
Jimmy Ryan
1052 Folsom St
San Francisco, CA 94103-2043
PH: (415) 703-8122
Fax: (415) 503-1633
jimmy@extremepizza.com
www.extremepizza.com,

Farmer Boys Food Inc.
restaurants
Don Tucker
3452 University Ave
Riverside, CA 92501

PH: (909) 275-9900
Fax: (909) 275-9930
dtucker@famerboys.com
www.farmerboys.com

Fastsigns
signs, and graphics services
Bill McPherson
2550 Midway Rd, Suite 150
Carrollton, TX 75006
Toll-Free: (800) 827-7446
Fax: (972) 248-8201
bill.mcpherson@fastsigns.com

FC Franchising Systems, Inc.
residential and commericial painting
10700 Montgomery Rd, Ste 300
Cincinnati, OH 45242-3296
PH: (800) 317-7089
Fax: (513) 587-4974
inquiry@freshcoatpainters.com
www.freshcoatpainters.com

Fiducial Franchises Inc.
accounting, payroll, tax, counseling
Howard Margolis
10480 Little Patuxent Pkwy,
    3rd floor
Columbia, MD, 21044-3568
PH: (800) 323-9000
Fax: (410) 910-5903
franchise@fiducial.com
www.fiducial.com

Fire Defense Centers, Inc.
sales and service of fire equipment
I. Larusso
6047 St Augustine Rd
Jacksonville, FL 32217-1200
PH: (904) 731-1833

First Interstate Inns
Jack L. Rediger, President
925 L Street
Lincoln, NE 68508-2229
PH: (402) 434-5620

Franchise Concepts Inc.
PO Box 1187
Houston, TX 77251-1187
PH: (281) 775-5262
Fax: (281) 872-1646
anance@fclbiz.com
www.thegreatframeup.com

**Frontier Publications, Inc. /
The Bingo Bugle Newspaper**
Vashon, WA 98070-0527
PH: (800) 327-6437
Fax: (206) 463-5630
tara@bigobugle.com
www.bingobugle.com

**Fun Bus Fitness Fun on
Wheels**
mobile fitness program
Kari Denton
32 Timothy Ln
Tinton Falls, NJ 07724-3134
PH: (732) 578-1287

Fax: (732) 389-7824
funbus@aol.com
www.funbus.com

Furniture Medic
furniture repair and restoration
Dinah Coopwood, Franchise
Lead Manager
3839 Forest Hill Ireno Rd
Memphis, TN 38125
PH: (800) 225-9687
Fax: (901) 597-7580
brwilliams@smclean.com
**www.
furnituremedicfranchise.com**

GC Franchising Systems, Inc.
coaching in self-employment
Franchise Department
10700 Montgomery Rd, Ste 300
Cincinnati, OH 45242-3296
PH: (888) 292-7992
Fax: (513) 563-4964
inquiry@thegrowthcoach.com
www.thegrowthcoach.com

Gelato Amare
homemade Italian ice cream
John Franklin, President
11504 Hyde Place
Raleigh, NC 27614-9626
PH: (919) 847-4435

Gill Associates

dental, medical and prescription
insurance

Don Gill
PO Box 591
Thorofare, NJ 08086-0591
PH: (856) 384-0440
Fax: (856) 384-0044
info@easylifeplus.com
www.easylifeplus.com
sales@gillassociates.com
www.easyshop4less.com

**Glass Doctor Auto Home
and Business, Glass Doctor
Corporation**

full-service glass replacement
providers in the nation with more
than 400 locations in the United
States and Canada

Mark Dawson, President
1020 N University Parks Dr
Waco, TX 76707-3858
PH: (800) 280-9959
Fax: (800) 378-9480
GlassDoctorFranchise@
DwyerGroup.com
**www.glassdoctor.com/
franchising**

Golden Corral Buffet & Grill

Larry I Tate, Senior Vice
President
PO Box 29502
Raleigh, NC 27626-0502

PH: (919) 881-5128
Fax: (919) 881-5252
ltate@goldencorral.net
www.goldencorral.com

Great Wraps, Inc.

hot wrapped sandwiches and
grilled subs

Dan Reed, Director of
Franchise Development
4 Executive Park East, Suite 315
Atlanta, GA 30329-2249
PH: (404) 248-9900 ext. 16
Fax: (404) 248-0180
franchise@greatwraps.com
www.greatwraps.com

Griswold Special Care

non-medical homecare

M. Patricia McLees
717 Bethlehem Pike, Suite 300
Erdenheim, PA 19038-8117
PH: (215) 402-0200
Fax: (215) 402-0202
mpatmclees@
griswoldspecialcare.com,
www.griswoldspecialcare.com

Grout Wizard

1056 El Capitan Dr
Danville, CA 94526-5463
PH: (925) 866-5000
Fax: (925) 552-6358
groutwizard@pacbell.net
www.groutwizard.com

Grove Recreation, Inc
miniature golf and family
entertainment centers
Charles H Grove, President
1207 Hillside Dr N
North Myrtle Beach, SC 29582
PH: (843) 249-2118
chgrove2001@aol.com

Gymboree Play Programs Inc.
children's programs
Franchise Development
500 Howard
San Francisco, CA 94105
PH: (800) 520-7529
Fax: (415) 278-7452
play_franchise@gymboree.com
www.gymboree.com

H.H. Franchising Systems Inc.
non-medical care
Franchise Department
10700 Montgomery Rd, Suite 300
Cincinnati, OH 45242-3296
Toll-Free: (800) 216-4196
Fax: (513) 563-2691
inquiry@homehelpers.cc
www.homehelpers.cc

Handyman Network
1165 E San Antonio Dr, Suite H
Long Beach, CA 90807-2374
Toll-Free: (888) 876-1148
Fax: (562) 216-9292
www.handyman-network.com

Hannoush Jewelers
Hannoush Franchise Corp.
134 Capital Dr
West Springfield, MA 01089
PH: (413) 846-4640
Fax: (413) 788-7588
www.hannoush.com

Happy & Healthy Products Inc.
home-based distribution business
for the wholesale and retail sale
of Fruitfull frozen fruit bars and
other items.
Susan Scotts
1600 S Dixie Hwy, Suite 200
Boca Raton, FL 33432
Toll-Free: (800) 764-6114,
Fax: (561) 368-5267
franchiseinfo@fruitfull.com
www.fruitfull.com

High Touch High Tech
Daniel Shaw, President
12352 Wiles RD
Coral Springs, FL 33076
PH: (954) 755-2900
Fax: (954) 755-1242
info@hightouch-hightech.com
www.nightouch-hightech.
com

Hilton Hotels Corp.
Franchise Department
9336 Civic Center Dr
Beverly Hills, CA 90210-3698
PH: (310) 278-4321
Fax: (310) 205-7655
www.hiltonfranchise.com

HobbyTown Unlimited Inc.
retail hobby stores
Nichole Ernst
6301 S 58th St
Lincoln, NE 68516-3676
Toll-Free: (800) 858-7370
Fax: (402) 434-5055
deo@hobbytown.com
www.hobbytown.com

House Doctors Handyman Service
handyman services
Franchise Department
575 Chamber Dr
Milford, OH 45150-1498
PH: (800) 319-3359
Fax: (513) 831-6010
www.housedoctors.com

House of Bread
Sheila McCann, President
858 Higuera St
San Luis Obispo, CA 93401
PH: (805) 542-0257
Toll-free PH: (800) 545-5146
Fax: (805) 542-0257

franchise@houseofbread.com,
www.houseofbread.com

Huntington Learning Centers, Inc.
Russ Miller
496 Kinderkamack Rd
Oradell, NJ 07649-1589
PH: (201) 261-8400
Fax: (201) 261-3233
franchise@huntingtonlearning
center.com
**www.huntingtonfranchise.
com**

IDQ Cos.
fast food franchiser
Development Department
7505 Metro Blvd
Minneapolis, MN 55439-3020
PH: (952) 830-0450
Fax: (952) 830-0450
www.dairyqueen.com

Ident-A-Kid Services of America Inc.
child safety
Rick Hagan
2810 Scherer Dr N, Suite 100
St Peterburg, FL 33716
PH: (727) 577-4646
Toll-Free: (800) 890-1000
Fax: (727) 576-8258
franchise@ident-a-kid.com
www.ident-a-kid.com

Intrivah Health and Wellness Intrivah Inc.
health and fitness franchise
Michael McConnell, Vice
President
2012 8th Ave
Altoona, PA 16602
Toll-Free: (800) 941-9251
Fax: (814) 941-8260
info@intrivah.com
www.intrivah.com

Isold It, LLC
eBay drop off stores
Ken Sully
129 N Hill Ave, Suite 202
Pasadena, CA 91106-1961
PH: (626) 584-0440
Fax: (626) 584-6540
www.i-soldit.com

It's a Grind Coffee House
coffee franchise
Steve Olsen
6272 E Pacific Coast Hwy
Suite E
Long Beach, CA 90803-4806
PH: (562) 594-5600
Fax: (562) 594-4100
www.tsagrind.com

Izzy's Franchise Systems, LLC
restaurant franchising
Franchise Department
PO Box 1689

Albany, OR 97321-0422
PH: (541) 926-8693
Fax: (541) 928-8127
Donac@izzyspizza.com
www.izzyspizza.com

J.W. Tumbles Licensing Corp.
Franchise Sales
Tanya Abel
312 S Cedros Ave, Suite 329
Solana Beach, CA 92130
PH: (858) 794-0484
www.jwtumbles.com

Kelly's Coffee & Fudge Factory
coffee franchising
Mary Gerlick
PO Box 21538
Bakersfield, CA 93390-1538
Toll-Free: (866) 462-6333
Fax: (661) 664-4785
info@kellyscoffee.com
www.kellyscoffee.com

Kitchen Solvers Inc.
cabinet refacing and kitchen remodeling
401 Jay St
La Crosse, WI 54601
PH: (608) 791-5516
Fax: (608) 784-2917
www.kitchensolvers.com

Kitchen Tune-up, KTU Worldwide Inc.
kitchen and bath services
Craig Green, Franchise Director
813 Circle Dr
Aberdeen, SD 57401
PH: (605) 225-4049
Fax: (605) 225-1371
ktu@kitchentuneup.com
www.kitchentuneup.com

The Krystal Company
Franchise Department
1 Union Square
Chattanooga, TN 37402
PH: (800) 458-5912
Fax: (423) 757-1588
cstringer@krystalco.com
www.krystal.com

La Paletera, La Paletera Franchise Systems Inc.
ice cream, fruit cup, and fruit bowl products
C Keith Hudson
3000 Weslayan St, Suite 108
Houston, TX 77027
PH: (713) 621-6200
Toll-free: (866) 621-6200
Fax: (713) 621-8200
seaboard07@aol.com
www.lapaletera.com

Labor Finders International Inc.
Chuck Woodweaver, Director of Franchise Development
3910 Rca Blvd, Suite 1001
Palm Beach Gardens, FL 33410
PH: (561) 627-6507
Fax: (561) 627-6556
robert.gallagher@laborfinders.com
www.laborfinders.com

Langenwalter Carpet Dyeing Langenwalter Industries Inc.
carpet dyeing and color restoration
1111 S Richfield Rd
Placentia, CA 92870
PH: (888) 526-4393
Fax: (714) 528-7620
info@langenwalter.com
www.langenwalter.com

Larry's Giant Sub
Larry Raikes, President
4479 Deerwood Lake Pkwy, Suite 1
Jacksonville, FL 32216
PH: (800) 358-6870
Fax: (904) 739-1218
www.larryssubs.com

The Laund-ur-mutt, Premier Pet Centers
Scott D Southworth, President
8854 Edgewood St
Highlands Ranch, CO 80130
PH: (303) 470-1540
muttman@laudurmutt.com
www.laudurmutt.com

Leisure Systems Inc.
Yogi Bear's Jellystone Parks
Rob Schutter, President
50 W Techne Center Dr, Suite G
Milford, OH 45150-9798
PH: (513) 232-6800
Fax: (513) 231-1191
rshutter@leisure-systems.com
www.campjellystone.com

Lesourd Associates
restaurant consultant
Chris LeSourd, President
3143 W Laurelhurst Dr NE
Seattle, WA 98105
PH: (206) 523-8037
(206) 523-0340
crlesourd@comcast.net
http://expert.expertpages.com/restaurantexpert

Little King Deli & Subs
Bob Wertheim
11811 I St
Omaha, NE 68137
PH: (402) 330-8019

Fax: (402) 330-3221
bob@littleking.us
www.littleking.us

Little Scientists Corp.
children's education services
14 Selden St
Woodbridge, CT 06525-2218
PH: (800) 322-8386
Fax: (203) 397-2165
dr-Heidi@little-scientists.com
www.little-scientists.com

The Living Light Weight Loss Program Inc.
weight loss hypnosis
2608 3rd Ave
Seattle, WA 98121
PH: (888) 246-6168
www.livinglitenow.com

Lotusea Wellness Group, Lotusea Franchising Group Inc.
Sandra Breeding
150 View Bend
Johnson City, TN 37601
PH: (423) 915-0852
Fax: (423) 282-1489
lotusea@hotmail.com
www.lotusea.com

Lox of Bagels
Adam Taylor, Vice President
11801 Prestwick Rd
Potomac, MD 20854-3631
PH: (301) 299-8523
www.bagelfranchises.com

Maid Brigade Inc.
Vice President of Franchise
Development
4 Concourse Pkwy NE, Ste 200
Atlanta, GA 30328
PH: (707) 551-9630
Fax: (770) 391-9092
www.maidbrigade.com

Maid Services of America
maid service
Tammy Spivey
475 E Main St, Suite 151
Cartersville, GA 30121-3353
PH: (770) 387-2455
Fax: (770) 382-0501
info@maidservicesofamerica.
com
www.maidservicesofamerica.com

Mail Boxes Etc
postal and business services
Franchise Sales
6060 Cornerstone Court West
San Diego, CA 92121
Toll-Free: (877) 623-7253
Fax: (858) 546-7493
www.theupsstore.com

Mats Floors & More
mats and matting
John C. Hoglund, President
978 E Hermitage Rd NE
Rome, GA 30161-9641
PH: (706) 295-4111
Fax: (706) 295-4114
jchoglund@yahoo.com
www.matsfloorsmore.com

**Mazzio's Italian Eatery,
Mazzio's Corporation**
Mark Long, Director,
Operation Services, Licensing,
4441 S 72nd East Ave
Tulsa, OK 74145
PH: (918) 663-8880
Toll-free: (800) 827-1910
Fax: (918) 641-1236
www.mazzios.com

McDonald's USA
Franchising Department
2915 Jorie Blvd
Oak Brook, IL 60523
Toll-Free: (888) 800-7257
Fax: (630) 623-5658
www.mcdonalds.com

Medipower
PO Box 335
San Marcos, TX 78667-0335
PH: (830) 629-1400
Fax: (512) 353-5333

Merry Maids
Franchise Sales Manager
PO Box 751017
Memphis, TN 38175-1017
PH: (800) 798-8000
Fax: (901) 597-8140
franchisesales@
mmhomeoffice.com
www.merrymaids.com

**Mighty Auto Parts,
Mighty Distributing System
of Americas, LLC**
*wholesale distribution of
automotive parts and products to
professional installers*
Barry Teagle
650 Engineering Dr
Norcross, GA 30092
PH: (770) 448-3900
Fax: (770) 446-8627
barry.teagle@mightautoparts.
com
www.mightyfranchise.com

Minute Man of America
restaurant franchising
James L Hansen, Owner
PO Box 828
Little Rock, AR 72203-0828
PH: (501) 666-8271

**Mr. Appliance, Expert
Appliance Repair — Mr.
Appliance Corporation**
*service and repair of all brands
of major household appliances
and repair of light commercial
equipment*
Doug Rogers, President
1020 N University Parks Dr.
Waco, TX 76707-3858
Toll-Free: (866) 903 4948
Toll-Free Fax: (800) 378-9480
MrApplianceFranchise@
DwyerGroup.com
**www.mrappliance.com/
franchising**

**Mr. Electric, Expert Electrical
Service, Mr. Electric
Corporation**
*mationwide electrical contracting
service franchise, serving the
needs of both residential and light
commercial users.*
Rick Cross, President
1020 N University Parks Dr.
Waco, TX 76707-3858
Toll-Free: (800) 253-9151
Toll-Free Fax: (800) 378-9480
MrElectricFranchise@
DwyerGroup.com
**www.mrelectric.com/
franchising**

Mr. Rooter Plumbing –
Mr. Rooter Corporation
residential and commercial
plumbing services
Mike Bidwell, President
1020 N University Parks Dr.
Waco, TX 76707-3858
Toll-Free: (800) 583-8003
Toll-Free Fax: (800) 378-9480
MrRooterFranchise@
DwyerGroup.com
www.mrrooter.com/
franchising

Mortgages and Loans
Unlimited, Broker One
Licensing Corp.
mortgage provider
Raymond A Strohl, President
1097 Irongate Lane, Suite C
Columbus, OH 43213
PH: (614) 864-1440

Moto Franchise Corporation
photography products and
services
Joe O'Hara
4444 Lake Center Dr
Dayton, OH 45426-3868
PH: (937) 854-6686 ext. 256
Fax: (937) 854-0140
johara@motophoto.com
www.motophoto.com

Moxie Java International, LLC
gourmet coffee, food, and gelato
Jack Spicer, Director of Sales
and Development
4990 W. Chinden Blvd
Boise, ID 83714
Toll-Free: (866) 676-6943
Fax: (208) 246-8525
franchise@moxiejava.com
www.moxiejava.com

Mr. Plant Inc.
interior landscape sales and
service
Larry McCarthy, Vice President
1106 2nd St
Encinitas, CA 92024-5008
PH: (800) 974-0488
Fax: (760) 295-5629
mrplant@cox.net
www.mrplant.com

Nat'l Restaurant Search Inc.
John W. Chitvanni, President
555 Sun Valley Dr, Suite J1
Roswell, GA 30076-5608
PH: (770) 650-1800
Fax: (630) 990-3131
john@restaurantheadhunter.
com
www.restaurantheadhunter.
com

Ness Studios
handpainted canvas oil portraits
from photos
Howard Ness, Owner/Director,
Dept FN
83 Scarcliffe Dr
Malverne, NY 11565
PH: (516) 593-2410
www.nessstudios.com

Next Step Franchising, Inc.
drycleaning
Laura Hurley, Franchise
Administrator
962 Washington St
Hanover, MA 02339-1613
Toll-Free: (866) 695-2735
Fax: (781) 829-9546
www.lapelsdrycleaning.com

Noble Roman Inc.
pizza and Tuscano's Italian Subs
restaurants
1 Virginia Ave, Suite 800
Indianapolis, IN 46204-3669
PH: (317) 634-3377
Fax: (317) 685-2294
pmobley@nobleromans.com
www.nobleromans.com

Norwalk – The Furniture Idea
furniture and retail
Mike Turbeville, Director of
Franchise
100 Furniture Pkwy

Norwalk, OH 44857
PH: (888) 667-9255
Fax: (419) 744-3212
mturbeville@nfcorp.com
**www.norwalkfurnitureidea.
com**

Nova Midia Inc.
cultural diversity testing and
racial attitude testing
Arne Rundquist, Sales
1724 N State St
Big Rapids, MI 49307
PH: (231) 796-4637
Fax: (231) 796-4637
www.novamediainc.com

**Oilstop Drive-thru Oil
Change, Oilstop Inc./Ps1 Inc.**
oil change and maintenance
service
Gary Woo
5665 Redwood Drive, Suite 6
Rohnert Park, CA 94928
PH: (707) 586-2047
Fax: (707) 586-2296
franchising@oilstopinc.com
www.oilstopinc.com

Olde World Tile Manufacturing, Olde World Enterprises Inc.
tile and stone manufacturing
John McKenzie Panagos, President
1517 Moccasin Creek Rd
Murphy, NC 28906
(828) 837-0357
Fax: (828) 837-1480
info@oldeworld.com
www.oldeworldtile.com

ORG Organization for the Home Division of Windquest Companies
Matt Hemmelgarn, National Sales
3311 Windquest Drive
Holland, MI 49424
PH: (616) 994-7638
matth@homeorg.com
www.homeorg.com

The Original Chicago Hoagie Hut
2807 Grand Ave
Waukegan, IL 60085
PH: (847) 249-8300
Fax: (847) 249-3190
www.hoagiehut.biz

Packing and Shipping Specialists
packaging, shipping, copying, and retail

Mike Gallagher
5211 85th, Suite 104
Lubbock, TX 79424
PH: (800) 877-8884, ext. 601,
Fax: (806) 794-9997
mike@packship.com
www.packship.com

Padgett Business Services
financial consulting, including payroll and taxes
160 Hawthorne Park
Athens, GA 30606-2147
Toll-Free PH: (800) 723-4388
Toll-Free Fax: (800) 548-1040
www.smallbixpros.com

Parker Interior
Rich Parker, President
1325 Terrill Rd
Scotch Plains, NJ 07076-2553
PH: (908) 322-5552
Fax: (908) 322-4818
rich@parkerplants.com
www.parkerplants.com

Paul Hastings Janofsky & Walker
Richard M Asbill, Partner
600 Peachtree St NE, Ste 2400
Atlanta, GA 30308
PH: (404) 815-2236
Fax: (404) 685-5236
rickasbill@paulhastings.com

Paul Revere's Pizza Int'l Ltd.
Larry Schuster, President
1570 42nd St NE
Cedar Rapids, IA 52402
PH: (319) 395-9113
Toll-free: (800) 995-9437
Fax: (319) 395-9115
larrys@paulrevesespizza.com,
www.paulreverespizza.com

Payless Car Rental System Inc.
automobile rental
2350 34th St N
St. Peterburg, FL 33713
PH: (727) 321-6352
Toll-free: (800) 729-5255
Fax: (727) 322-6540
franchise@paylesscarrental.com
www.paylesscarrental.com

Payz Inc.
payroll and bookkeeping services
John Rogers, Manager of
Franchise Development
4102 42nd Ave S
Minneapolis, MN 55406
PH: (800) 999-6633
Fax: (612) 729-0990
agent@payz.com
www.payz.com

Peggy Lawton Kitchens Inc.
bakery route
William Wolf, Vice President/
General Manager

PO BOX 33
East Walpole, MA 02032
Toll-Free: (800) 843-7325

Penn Station Inc.
Mark Partusch, Director of
Sales
8276 Beechmont Ave
Cincinnati, OH 45255-3153
PH: (513) 474-5957
Fax: (513) 474-7116
www.penn-station.com

Pepe's Mexican Restaurant
Edwin Ptak, Franchise
Director
1325 W 15th St
Chicago, IL 60608
PH: (312) 733-2500
Fax: (312) 733-2564
info@pepes.com
www.pepes.com

Personal Best Karate
Christopher Rappold
250 E Main St
Norton, MA 02766-2436
PH: (508) 285-5425
Fax: (781) 285-7064
founder@personalbestkarate.
com
www.personalbestkarate.com

Pigtails & Crewcuts

children's hair salon
Michelle Holliman
1100 Old Ellis Rd, Suite 600
Roswell, GA 30076-4993
PH: (877) 752-6800
Fax: (770) 752-8880
**www.Pigtailsandcrewcuts.
com**

Pillar to Post Professional Home Inspection

home inspection services
Jim Majirsky, Director of
Franchise Development
13902 N Dale Mabry Hwy
   Suite 300
Tampa FL 33618
Toll-Free: (877) 963-3129
Fax: (813) 963-5301
franchise.development@
pillartopost.com
www.pillartopost.com

Practical Rent-A-Car Systems, Inc.

car and truck rentals
Robert Barton, Executive Vice
President
4780 I 55 N, Suite 300
Jackson, MS 39211-5583
PH: (601) 713-4333
Fax: (601) 782-9850
www.usave.com

Professional Referral Exchange

networking organization
Eve Peterson, President
125 Hivue Lane
Pittsburgh, PA 15237
Toll-Free: (800) 929-5323
Fax: (412) 761-8584
pre@prorefx.com
www.propefx.com

Property Damage Appraisers, Inc.

*insurance and risk management
inspections*
Rodney Caudill, Vice
President-Marketing
6100 SW Blvd, Suite 200
Benbrook, TX 76109-3964
Toll-Free: (800) 749-7324
Fax: (817) 731-5565
rodney.caudill@pdaorg.net
www.pdahomeoffice.com

Quicksilver International Inc.

Bill King
618 State St
Bristol, TN 37621
PH: (423) 764-2686
Fax: (423) 764-0234

Racing Limos Inc.
advertising, automotive, and
transportation
David Ziccarelli
5621 Strand Blvd #205
Naples, FL 34110
Toll-Free: (866) 746-5466
Fax: (239) 513-2209
mall@racinglimos.com
www.racinglimos.com

**Rainbow International
Restoration & Cleaning,
Rainbow International
Corporation**
a full-service restoration and
cleaning business.
David Bethea, President
1020 N University Parks Dr.
Waco, TX 76707-3858
PH: (800) 583-9100
Fax: (800) 378-9480
RainbowFranchise@
DwyerGroup.com
**www.rainbowintl.com/
franchising**

Reading Friends Franchise Co.
Nancy Spencer, CEO
5228 Pershing Ave
Fort Worth, TX 76107
PH: (817) 738-9430
Fax: (817) 732-2079
nancyspencer@
readingfriends.org,
www.readingfriends.org

Receil It International Inc.
commercial ceiling cleaning
Glenn Scheel, Franchise Director
175B Liberty St
Copiague, NY 11726-1207
PH: (631) 842-0099
Fax: (631) 980-7668
info@receilit.com,
www.receilit.com

Red Wing Shoes
314 Main St
Red Wing, MN 55066-2337
PH: (651) 388-8211
Fax: (651) 388-8211
www.redwingshoes.com

Resort Maps Franchise Inc.
Peter Hans, Franchise Director
PO Box 726
Waitsfield, VT 05673-0726
PH: (802) 496-6877
Fax: (802) 496-6278
peter@resortmaps.com
www.resortmaps.com

Rightlook.com
auto detailing and paint touch-
up, dent repair
Stephen Powers
7616 Miramar Rd #5300
San Diego, CA 92126-4202
PH: (858) 271-4271
Fax: (858) 271-4303
requestinfo@rightlook.com
www.rightlook.com

Rollerz Kahala Corp.
7730 E. Greenway Rd., Ste 104
Scottsdale, AZ 85260
PH: (480) 443-0200
Fax: (480) 443-1972

SRA International Inc.
Brent Nixon, Vice President
and Franchise Director
3737 Embassy Pkwy, Suite 200
Akron, OH 44333-8369
PH: (800) 731-7724
bnnixon@sanfordrose.com
www.sanfordrose.com

Safe Kids Card Inc.
child, adult and pet identification
services
Jeremiah Hutchins, Sales
Manager
17100 Bear Valley Rd #238
Victorville, CA 92395-5852
PH: (760) 486-1506
Fax: (760) 249-5751
www.myfamilycd.com

Safe-Stride International Inc.
slip-resistant floor products
R.E. Colfels, President
6549 Golden Horshoe Dr
Seminole, FL 33777
Toll-Free: (800) 646-3005
Fax: (727) 399-0188
motik@tampabay.rr.com
www.safe-stride-
international.com

Salsbury Industries
Director of Marketing
1010 E 62nd St
Los Angeles, CA 90001-1510
Toll-Free: (800) 725-7287
www.salsbury.com

Sampa Corp.
printing, copying, packing, and
shipping services
Joe Collins, Sales Director
852 Broadway, Suite 300
Denver, CO 80203-2700
Toll-Free: (800) 852-6336
(303) 779-8445
info@signalgraphics.com
www.signalgraphics.com

San Francisco Oven, SFO
Franchise Development Ltd
Matt Harper, CEO
9150 S Hills Blvd, Suite 225
Cleveland, OH 44147
PH: (440) 717-9450
Fax: (440) 717-9447
mharper@sonfrancisooven.com
www.sanfranciscooven.com

Scallopini Ventures
1650 E 12 Mile Rd
Madison Heights, MI
    48071-2679
PH: (248) 542-3281
Fax: (248) 542-7660
salscal12@sbgglobal.net
www.salvatorescallopini.com

Scotts Lawn Service
lawn care
Shayne Gargala, Franchise
Development Manager
14111 Scottslawn Rd
Marysville, OH 43041
PH: (800) 221-1760, ext. 5641
shayne.gargala@scotts.com
www.scottslawnservice.com

Seaga Manufacturing Corp.
vending equipment
700 Seaga Dr
Freeport, IL 61032-9644
PH: (813) 297-9500
Fax: (815) 297-1700
info@seagamfg.com
www.seagamfg.com

Sentry Technologies, LLC
Brian C. Famous, President
PO Box 1022
Bensalem, PA 19020-5022
PH: (610) 906-1582
Fax: (610) 906-3369
info@sentrykids.com
www.sentrykids.com

Sign Biz Inc.
sign shops
Greg Salzane, Vice President
24681 La Piz, Suite 270
Dana Point, CA 92629-2592
Toll-Free: (800) 633-5580
Fax: (949) 234-0426

gregs@signbiz.com
www.signbiz.com

Signature Landscape Lighting
outdoor lighting products
Bob Borai
PO Box 355
Novi, MI 48376-0355
PH: (248) 347-1117
Fax: (248) 344-1761
signature@core.com
www.signaturelights.com

Sir Speedy Inc.
*printing, copying, and mailing
services*
Randall Lorp
26722 Plaza Dr
PO Box 9077
Mission Viejo, CA 92691-6390
PH: (949) 348-5000
Fax: (949) 348-5066
success@sirspeedy.com
www.sirspeedy.com

Small Business Club
Marketing Director
PO Box 2440
Midland, MI 48641-2440
Toll-Free: (800) 457-7973
Fax: (989) 496-2551
sbc@universal-os.com
www.isp-income.com

Smokey P Inc.
Cleatrice Price, President
1134 Groves Dr
Rockledge, FL 32955-2223
PH: (321) 639-0038
Fax: (321) 639-4318
smokeyp@digital.net
www.digital.net/mr-bbq

Snap-On Company
Franchise Department
2801 80th St
Kenosha, WI 53143-5699
Toll-Free: (877) 476-2766
Fax: (262) 656-5088
www.snapon.com

Snelling Staffing Services
Snelling Services LLC
full service staffing
12801 N Central Expy, Ste 600
Dallas, TX 75243
Toll-Free: (800) 766-5556
Fax: (972) 383-3839
sales@snelling.com
www.snelling.com

Solid/Flue Chimney Systems Inc.
chimney lining and restoration
Doug La Fleur, President
4937 Starr St SE
Grand Rapids, MI 49546-7934
PH: (616) 940-8809
chimney@solidflue.com
www.solidflue.com

Sparkle Wash
Sparkle International Inc.
pressure washing and restoration
Thomas Yuhas, Vice President
26851 Richmond Rd
Cleveland, OH 44146
Toll-Free: (800) 321-0770
Fax: (216) 464-8869
yuhas@sparklewash.com
www.sparklewash.com

Spring Green Lawn Care Corp.
11909 S.Spaulding School Dr.
Plainfield, IL 60585-9501
Toll-Free: (800)777-8608
Fax: (215) 659-3227, ext. 9800
www.chernowkatz.com

Stardek
Lisa Simmons
928 Sligh Ave
Seffner, FL 33584-3142
PH: (813) 655-4880
Fax: (813) 655-8830
info@stardek.com
www.stardek.com

Steak Escape, The
Escape Enterprises Ltd.
Lloyd Allen
222 Neilston St
Columbus, OH 43215
PH: (614) 224-0300
Fax: (614) 224-6460
lallen@steakescape.com
www.steakescape.com

Steak & Shake Company, The Franchise Development
500 Century Building
36 S Pennsylvania St
Indianapolis, IN 46204-3630
PH: (317) 633-4100
Fax: (317) 633-4105
www.steaknshake.com

Stork News Of America
birth announcements
stork rentals
1305 Hope Mills Rd
Fayetteville, NC 28304
PH: (800) 633-6395
Fax: (910) 426-2473
jayjy@storknews.com

SuperCoups
Bill Matthews, Vice President
350 Revolutionary Drive
East Taunton, MA 2718
PH: (508) 977-2000
Fax: (508) 977-0644
www.supercoups.com

Superglass Windshield Repair Inc.
David A. Casey, President
6101 Chancellor Dr, Suite 200
Orlando, FL 32809-5672
PH: (407) 240-1920
Fax: (407) 240-3266
david@sgwr.com
www.sgwr.com

Superslow Zone, LLC
health and fitness
Madeline Ross
285 W Central Pkwy, Ste 1726
Altamonte Springs, FL
   32714-2579
PH: (407) 937-0050
Fax: (407) 937-0431
mross@superslowzone.com
www.superslowzone.com

Surface Specialists Systems Inc.
bathroom and kitchen remodeling
alternatives, including repair,
refinishing, and acrylic liners
Amy Irali, Marketing and
Sales Director
621 Stallings Rd, Suite B
Matthews, NC 28104
PH: (704) 821-3380
Fax: (704) 821-2097
amy@surfacespecialists.com
www.surfacespecialists.com

Taco John's International Inc.
Dr. Brett Miller
808 W 20th St
Cheyenne, WY 82001-3404
PH: (800) 854-0819, ext. 9107
Fax: (307) 772-0369
bmiller@tacojohns.com
www.tacojohns.com

Taco Mayo Franchise Systems Inc.
Debbie Jackson, Franchise Qualification Specialist
10405 Greenbriar Place
Oklahoma City, OK 73159-7636
PH: (405) 691-8226
Fax: (405) 691-2572
www.tacomayo.com

Taco Palace National Franchise LLC
Mexican fast food
Matt Deves
PO Box 87
Monett, MO 65708
PH: (573) 216-1739
2nd PH: (417) 235-6595
Fax: (417) 235-1150
matt@tacopalace.com
www.tacopalace.com

Thrifty Rent-A-Car System Inc.
Coordinator, Karen Peacock
5310 E 31st St
Tulsa, OK 74135-5073
PH: (918) 669-2219
Fax: (918) 669-2061
franchisesales@thrifty.com
www.thrifty.com

Tubby's Grilled Submarines, Tubby's Sub Shops Inc.
submarine sandwiches
Jennifer Ciampa
35807 Moravian Dr
Clinton Twp, MI 48035
PH: (586) 792-2369
Fax: (586) 792-4250
jennifer@tubby.com
www.tubby.com

Turbo Leadership Systems Franchise Department
leadership training
36280 NE Wilsonville Rd
Newberg, OR 97132-7105
Toll-Free: (800) 574-4373
Fax: (503) 625-2699
turbo@
turboleadershipsystems.com
www.
turboleadershipsystems.com

Typing Tigers
Manager
PO Box 828
San Marcos, TX 78667-0008
PH: (830) 629-1400

Ultrasonics
ultrasonic cleaning systems
Stan Morantz, President
9984 Gantry Rd
Philadelphia, PA 19115-1076
Toll-Free: (800) 695-4522
Fax: (215) 969-0566
info@morantz.com
**www.ultrasonicsmachines.
com**

**United States Basketball
League**
professional basketball
46 Quirk Rd
Milford, CT 06460-3745
PH: (203) 877-9508
Fax: (203) 878-8109
usbl96@aol.com
www.usbl.com

Uniway Management Corp.
*buying service showroom and
design center home furnishings*
Robert C. Hardy
5182A Old Dixie Hwy
Forest Park, GA 30297
PH: (404) 363-6200
Fax: (404) 363-8848
uniway@bellsouth.net
www.uniway.com

Us Structures Inc./Archadeck
*remodeling and construction
services*
Pete Wiggins, President CEO
2112 W Laburnum Ave, Ste 100
Richmond, VA 23227-4358
PH: (804) 353-6999
Fax: (804) 358-1878
petew@ussi.net
www.archadeck.com

V2K Window Décor & More
Victor Yosha, President
1127 Auraria Pkwy Unit 204
Denver, CO 80204-1899
PH: (303) 202-1120
Fax: (303) 202-5201
Vic@v2k.com
www.v2k.com

**Victory Lane Quick Oil
Change**
*oil change and maintenance
services*
Earl W. Farr, Director of
Franchise Sales
405 Little Lake Dr
Ann Arbor, MI 48103-6220
PH: (734) 996-1196
Fax: (734) 996-4912
www.victorylane.net

VideoMasters Inc.
video production
Rory Graham
2200 Dunbarton Dr, Suite D
Chesapeake, VA 23325
PH: (800) 836-9461
Fax: (757) 424-8693
corporate@
videomasteronline.com
www.videomasters.inc

**Water Resources
International**
air and water services
Lowell E Foletta, President
2800 E Chambers St
Poenix, AZ 85040
PH: (602) 268-2580, ext. 1202
Fax: (602) 268-8080

**We Must Be Nuts!!!
Distributors Of Kish and
Molnar Enterprises Inc.**
*cinnamon roasted nut
distributorship*
Glenn C Kish, President
PO Box 813
Clarcona, FL 32710
PH: (407) 672-3609
Fax: (352) 536-9886
nuttycoon6@aol.com
www.kish-distributors.com

**West Coast Commercial
Credit & Investments**
*re-sales, new site development
and appraisal financing*
President, Gary D Anderson
PO Box 19241
San Diego, CA 92159
PH: (800) 804-7901
Fax: (619) 280-2575
franchisebroker@att.net
franchise.financing@att.net

White Hen Pantry Inc.
Tangy McGee
700 E. Butterfield Rd, Suite 300
Lombard, IL 60148
PH: (630) 366-3100
Toll-free: (800) 726-8791
Fax: (630) 366-3447
tangy.mcgee@whitehen.com
www.whitehen.com

**Wholly Crap LLC Franchising
Unlimited**
pet waste removal service
Dave Hillman
392 Seaburn St
Brookfield, OH 44403
Toll-Free: (800) 929-0808
www.whollycrap.com

Wildlife Management Supplies
9435 E Cherry Bend Rd
Traverse City, MI 49684-7618
Toll-Free: (800) 451-6544
Fax: (231) 947-9440
info@crittercontrol.com
www.crittercontrol.com

Winch Enterprises
parking-lot cleanup
Brian Winch, Owner
227 Bellevue Way NE Pmb 249
Bellevue, WA 98004-5721
PH: (403) 236-7551
Fax: (403) 246-0582
www.cleanlots.com

Window Works International Inc.
Scott Thompson, President
3601 Minnesota Dr, Ste 800
Edina, MN 55435-5250
PH: (952) 943-4353
Fax: (651) 690-1464
info@windowworks.net
www.windowworks.net

Winger's Franchising Inc.
Eric Slaymaker, President
404 E 4500 S, Suite A12
Salt Lake City, UT 84107-2777
PH: (801) 261-3700
Fax: (801) 261-1615
www.wingers.info

Wireless Toyz
cellular superstore
Gail Parker
23399 Commerce Drive, Ste b-1
Farmington Hills, MI
    48335-2763
Toll-Free: (866) 237-2624, ext. 111
Fax: (248) 671-0346
franchise@wirelesstoyz.com
www.wirelesstoyz.com

Wood Re New
clean and protect decks, docks, fences, cedar and redwood siding
Stan Krempges
220 S Dysart Ave
Springfield, MO 65802
PH: (417) 833-3303
Fax: (417) 833-5479
stan@woodrenew.com
www.woodrenew.com

Woodcraft Franchise Corporation
woodworking supply specialty store
William T. Carroll, Director of Franchising
1177 Rosemar Rd
Parkersburg, WV 26105
PH: (304) 422-5412
Fax: (304) 485-1938
www.woodcraft.com

Woodplay Family Industries
redwood playsets
Franchise Department
Janet Kennedy
2101 Harrod St
Raleigh, NC 27604
PH: (919) 875-4499
Fax: (919) 875-4256
www.woodplay.com

WRPC Inc.
handrolled soft pretzels
President, Kevin Krabill
2500 W State St
Alliance, OH 44601-5605
PH: (330) 823-0575
Fax: (330) 821-8908
kkrabill@wererolling.com
www.wererolling.com

**Wyane R. Irwin Trust, Global
Domain International**
Wayne R. Irwin
4609 Meadowood Dr
Baytown, TX 77521
PH: (281) 424-7651
Fax: (281) 424-7676
wirwin7418@aol.com
**www.movie.ws/wayne1935/
show**

**Young Rembrandts
Franchise Inc.**
a children's drawing program
Kim Swanson, Director of
Franchise Operations
23 N Union St
Elgin, IL 60123
PH: (847) 742-6966
Toll-free: (866) 300-6030
Fax: (847) 742-7197
yr@youngrembrandts.com
www.youngrembrandts.com

FRANCHISE ATTORNEYS AND SERVICE PROVIDERS

Thiis is a partial, random listing of franchise lawyers. They are listed in alphabetical order by state showing company name, contact title, contact name, address, city, state, ZIP, phone number one, phone number two (if available), fax, e-mail, Web site and type of franchise.

Arizona

International Mergers & Acquisitions Inc.
consulting services
Neil D. Lewis, President
4300 N Miller Rd, Suite 230
Scottsdale, AZ 85251-3622
PH: (480) 990-3899
Fax: (480) 990-7480
nlewis@ima-world.com
www.ima-world.com

Gust Rosenfeld Plc
John L. Hay, Lawyer
201 E Washington St, Suite 800
Phoenix AZ 85004
PH: (602) 257-7468
Fax: (602) 254-4878
jhay@gustlaw.com
www.gustlaw.com

California

Leon Gottlieb & Associates
restaurant and franchise consultant
4601 Sendero Place
Tarzana, CA 91356-4821
PH: (818) 757-1131
Fax: (818) 757-1816
lgottlieb@aol.com
www.members.aol.com/ lgottlieb/myhomepage/ business.html

American Association of Franchisees & Dealers
association
Robert Purvin Jr., CEO
P.O. Box 81887
San Diego, CA 92138-1887,
PH: (619) 209-3775
Fax: (619) 209-3777
benefits@aafd.org
www.aafd.org

Franchisee Legaline

American Association of Franchisees & Dealers

Stacie Power, Member Services
PO Box 81887
San Diego CA 92138-1887
PH: (800) 733-9858
Fax: (619) 209-3777
benefits@aafd.org
www.aafd.org

Colorado

Law Offices of Van Elmore
Van Elmore, Principal
600 17th St, Suite 2800
South Denver, CO 80202-5402
PH: (303) 659-7342
Fax: (303) 659-1051
velmore@elmorelaw.com
www.elmorelaw.com

Florida

Franchise Development International LLC
franchise consulting
Linda Biciocchi
370 SE. 15th Ave
Pompano Beach, FL 33060-7624
PH: (954) 942-9424
Fax: (954) 783-5177
fdiintl@bellsouth.net
www.fdiintl.com

Hawaii

Business Brokers Hawaii, LLC.
Assisting clients with converting to a franchise business mode
Milton Docktor, Founder-President
3230 Pikai Way
Wailea, HI 96753-7702
PH: (808) 879-8833
Fax: (808) 879-5966
mdr@business-brokers.com
www.business-brokers.com

Illinois

Franchise Architects
Craig S. Slavin, President
2275 Half Day Rd, Suite 350
Bannockburn, IL 60015-1277
PH: (847) 465-3400
Fax: (847) 821-2610
info@franchisearchitects.com,
www.franchisearchitects.com

Carter & Tani
Doris Adkins Carter and
Christine K. Tani, Partners
402 E Roosevelt Rd, Suite 206
Wheaton, IL 60187-5588
PH: (630) 668-2135
Fax: (630) 668-9009
cartani@cartertani.com
www.cartertani.com

Indiana

Environmental Assessments Franchise
217 East Main Street
Brownsburg, IN 46112-1418
PH: (317) 852-7765
Toll-Free: (800) 891-8582

Ice Miller LLP
Ruth Reese
1 American Square, Suite 3100
Indianapolis, IN 46282-0200
PH: (317) 236-2100
www.icemiller.com

Kentucky

Frost Brown Todd LLC
Robert Y. Gwin, Partner
400 W. Market St, Suite 3200
Louisville, KY 40202-3363
PH: (502) 589-5400
rgwin@fbtlaw.com
www.frostbrowntodd.com

Massachusetts

McGrow Consulting
full service franchise consulting firm
Jack McBirney, President
30 North St
Hingham, MA 00204-2240
Toll-Free: (800) 358-8011
Fax: (781) 740-2287
mcgrow@mcgrow.com
www.mcgrow.com

McKenna Associates Corp.
franchise and business consulting
Jim McKenna, President
52 Crestview Rd
Milton, MA 02186-3638
PH: (617) 333-4967
Toll-Free: (866) 425-4338
jfmmac@comcast.net
www.mckennaassociatescorp. com

Weston, Patrick, Willard & Reddiing
L. Seth Stadfeld, Member
84 State St
Boston, MA 02109-2299
PH: (617) 742-9310
Fax: (617) 742-5734
www.franchise-counsel.com

Minnesota

Larkin Hoffman Daly & lindgren Ltd.
law firm representing franchisers
Charles S. Modell
7900 Xerxes Ave S
1500 Wells Fargo Plaza
Minneapolis, MN 55431-1006
PH: (952) 896-3341
Fax: (952) 896-1511
cmodell@larkinhoffman.com
www.larkinhoffman.com

Missouri

Armstrong Teasdale LLP
Edward R. Spalty, Partner
2345 Grand Blvd., Suite 2000
Kansas City, MO 64108-2617
PH: (816) 221-3420
Toll-free: (800) 243-5070
Fax: (816) 221-0786
espalty@armstrongteasdale.
com
www.armstrongteasdale.com

North Carolina

Kushell Associates Inc.
Bob Kushell, President
235 Fearrington Post
Pittsboro, NC 27312-8555
PH: (919) 542-3500
Fax: (919) 542-1156
kushellassociates@msn.com
www.kushellassociates.com

New Jersey

Mitchell J. Kassoff Franchise,
legal representation of franchisers and franchisees in all 50 states
Mitchell Kassoff
2 Foster Court
South Orange, NJ 07079-1002
PH: (973) 762-1776
franchiselawyer@verizon.net
www.franatty.cnc.net

Hospitality Solutions LLC
franchise agreement formulation and franchise agreement termination negotiations
Steve Belmonte, Attorney, Owner
3 Golden Corner Way
Randolph, NJ 07869-3490
PH: (973) 598-0839
Fax: (973) 927-4082,
Stevenbelmonte@aol.com
www.stevenbelmonte.com

New York

Pitegoff Law Office
Attorney at Law, Tom Pitegoff
10 Bank St, Suite 540
White Plains, NY 10606-1952
PH: (914) 681-0100
fax (914) 206-6003
pitegoff@pitlaw.com
www.pitlaw.com

Ohio

Luce Smith & Scott Inc.
business insurance programs for franchises
6880 W Snowville Rd, Ste 220
Cleveland, OH 44141-3255
PH: (440) 746-1700
Fax: (440) 746-1130
jmdwyer@lucesmithscott.com

John R. Mohr, Attorney
201 E. 6th St
Dayton, OH 45402
PH: (937) 913-0200

**Relo Franchise Services/
Relocation Strategies**
Timothy Haines
17 E 8th St, Suite 100
Cincinnati, OH 45202-2001
PH: (513) 651-2332
Fax: (513) 651-0860
info@relocationstrategies.net
www.relocationstrategies.net

Pennsylvania

Franchise International Inc.
Ken Franklin, President
4730 Centre Ave
Pittsburgh, PA 15213-1759
PH: (412) 687-8484
Fax: (412) 687-0541
franchise-inc@earthlink.net

Chernow Katz LLC
Harris Chernow, Esquire
721 Dresher Rd, Suite 1100
Horsham, PA 19044
PH: (215) 659-3600
Fax: (215) 659-3227
hcharmnow@
chernowkatz.com
www.chernowkatz.com

Texas

**Seaboard Franchise Services
Company**
franchise consulting firm
Keith Hudson
3000 Weslayan St, Suite 108
Houston, TX 77027-5739
PH: (713) 621-6200
Toll-free: (866) 621-6200
Fax: (713) 621-8200
mail@saboardfranchise.com
www.seaboardfranchise.com

**Nationwide Franchise
Marketing Services**
Marvin J. Migdol, Owner
18715 Gibbons Dr
Dallas, TX 75287-4045
PH: (972) 733-9942
Fax: (972) 335-6581
mmigdol@careington.com
franchise development

Virginia

Piper Rudnick Gray Gary U.S. LLP

franchise law
Bret Lowell, Partner
1775 Wlehle Ave, Suite 400
Reston, VA 20190-5159
PH: (703) 773-4242
Fax: (703) 773-5053
bret.lowell@dlapiper.com
www.dlapiper.com

Williams Mullen

Warren Lewis, Partner
8270 Greensboro Dr, Suite 700
Mclean, VA 22102-3835
PH: (703) 760-5228
Toll-Free: (888) 783-8181
Fax: (703) 748-0244
wlewis@williansmullen.com
www.williamsmullen.com

Washington

Bundy & Morrill Inc. Ps.

legal services for franchisers and franchisees
Howard E. Bundy
12351 Lake City Way NE,
    Suite 202
Seattle, WA 98125-5437
PH: (206) 367-4640
Fax: (206) 367-5507
bundy@bundymorrill.com
www.bundymorrill.com

Dorsey & Whitney LLP

Gary R. Duvall, Shareholder
1420 5th Ave.
Seattle, WA 98101-4087
PH: (206) 903-8700
Fax: (206) 903-8820
duvall.gary@dorsey.com
www.dorsey.com

Atlantic Publishing has exhaustively searched for companies that provide franchise products and/or services. This is a comprehensive listing to help our readers find companies and products. Listings are alphabetical. We have provided Web sites and e-mail addresses if available.

Help us help you! If you know some data that has changed or know of a company that should be listed, please use the form below and contact us via our toll free fax at 877-682-7819.

Edit directory of franchise businesses and/or attorneys

❑ Please add a new listing
❑ Please edit/append my listing on page # _____

Your Name: _____

Organization Name: _____

Address: _____

_____

City: _____ State: _____ Zip: _____

Telephone:_____ Fax: _____

Web site URL: _____

E-mail Address: _____

Comments: _____

_____

_____

Please fax this form to 877-682-7819

Glossary

A

ACCOUNTING PERIOD A period of time, such as a quarter or year, for which a financial statement is produced.

ACCOUNTS PAYABLE Amounts owed to providers and creditors by a business.

ACCOUNTS RECEIVABLE Money that is owed to a company by customers who have bought goods and services on credit.

ACKNOWLEDGEMENT OF RECEIPT Signed record that shows the acceptance of documents or product on a particular date.

ADVERTISING FEE An annual fee paid to the franchiser for any advertising costs.

AGGREGATE PAR VALUE The par value multiplied by the number of authorized shares; this amount is important in determining initial fees and annual franchise taxes in many states.

AGREEMENT A contract signed with a franchiser; also called the Franchise Agreement.

AMBIANCE Sounds, sights, smells and attitude of an operation.

ANCHOR TENANT A tenant strategically positioned to produce a vast quantity of consumers.

ANNUAL MEETING OF SHAREHOLDERS A meeting held once a year for shareholders to elect executive positions and vote on company issues.

ANNUAL REPORT A yearly report naming administrators,

members, and providing financial information.

APPROVED PRODUCTS
Products that are approved by the franchiser for the franchisee to purchase.

ARBITRATION A process for settling disputes between parties that is less structured than court proceedings.

AREA DEVELOPMENT RIGHTS The right to open a quantity of franchises in a defined area approved by the franchiser.

AREA EFFICIENCY Calculation of sales level obtained in an area.

AREA FRANCHISE A franchise that develops accompanying franchise sites within a defined region.

ARTICLES OF INCOR- PORATION Documents required by law to start a corporation that contain information about the company.

ASSESSOR A person who estimates the value of property for the purpose of taxation.

ASSET Everything owned by a company that has profitable or redeemable value.

ASSUMED NAME The non- legal or trade name that the corporation uses to conduct business.

AUDIT Authentication of financial records and accounting procedures.

AUTHORIZED SHARES OR STOCK A specified number of shares defined in the articles of incorporation that a corporation is allowed to issue.

B

BALANCE SHEET A financial statement that reports a company's assets and liabilities at a specific point in time.

BANK NOTE A note issued by a bank that must be paid back upon demand; used as money.

BANKRUPTCY A financial state when a company is no longer in control of its money.

BOARD OF DIRECTORS A group of people elected by the shareholders to manage and set company policies.

BOTTOM-UP BUDGET Secondary employees prepare a budget and then send it to upper management for approval.

BREAK-EVEN POINT The point at which no profit is made because the sales equal the costs.

BUSINESS ENTITY An organization that possesses a separate existence for tax reasons.

BUSINESS FORMAT FRANCHISE A format the franchiser sets up so that the franchisee can use the products, service and trademarks of the franchiser.

BUSINESS PLAN A plan that explains the vision, objectives, needs and necessary steps to become a successful business; a plan that provides the objects of a business and the steps necessary to achieve those objectives.

BUSINESS PROFILE A business description and definition.

BUY-SELL AGREEMENT A written agreement between a borrower, short-term lender and permanent lender that assigns the mortgage to the permanent lenders after construction is completed.

BYLAWS A corporation's internally elected rules made to regulate what each individual's role will be and establishes procedures for conducting business.

C

C-CORPORATION A corporation that is taxed under the Internal Revenue Code

Section II and subchapter C.

CAPITAL Any cash, funds, assets and accounts that the business currently possesses.

CAPITAL REQUIRED The amount of resources needed to establish a franchise.

CAPITALIZATION RATE A percentage of the investment that is the desired return in the business.

CASH ACCOUNTING A form of accounting where expenses are not considered until they are paid and income is considered earned when it is received.

CASH FLOW CONTROL Foretelling your potential requirements for cash.

CERTIFICATE OF INSURANCE Proof of insurance coverage.

CHAIN OF COMMAND A series of management positions in order of authority.

CHURNING When franchisers take back failed locations and remarket them repeatedly.

CLOSELY HELD CORPORATION Family members or very few people actually hold shares with the corporation.

COLLATERAL Used to

guarantee a creditor an asset that can be sold for cash.

COMMODITY BUSINESS A business that competes primarily on the basis of price.

COMMON STOCK An equity investment that represents ownership in a company.

COMPANY-OWNED OUTLET A company-owned store that is identical to the franchised stores.

COMPOUND INTEREST Interest charged on the principal in addition to the accumulated interest.

CONSUMER ORIENTATION The needs of consumers determine management decisions.

CONTRACT An arrangement in which two or more parties agree to terms.

CONVERSION FRANCHISE An independent business that joins a national franchise to use its name and trademark.

COPYRIGHT Exclusive right of a person to use and license others to use their work.

CORPORATE SEAL A device that contains the company's information that is embossed or imprinted onto corporate documents.

CURRENT LIABILITY Debts owed that are payable in less than 12 months.

D

DEFAULT A breach of contract; failure to pay on a promissory note when due.

DELAYED EFFECTIVE DATE The date when the corporation will be officially recognized by the state.

DENOMINATOR Common trait or standard.

DEPRECIATION Decrease in value of a long-term asset over time.

DESIGNATED SUPPLIER Franchiser's chosen supplier for purchased products.

DIRECTORS People responsible for determining the policy of a corporation or entity; usually elected by the shareholders.

DISCLOSURE DOCUMENT A document that allows prospective franchisees to evaluate the company.

DISTRIBUTORSHIP A right granted by a manufacturer or wholesaler to sell a product to others.

DIVIDEND Distribution of a company's profit to shareholders.

DOMAIN NAME A name that distinguishes a company from other companies on the Internet.

DOMESTIC CORPORATION A corporation in a state where it was incorporated.

DUE DILIGENCE Examining financial records and other business information before taking a business opportunity.

E

EARNINGS CLAIMS The franchisee's sales, profit, and other financial information declared by the franchiser.

EBITDA Earnings Before Interest, Taxes, Depreciation, and Amortization: A measure of cash flow.

E-COMMERCE The way business is done online, by selling and receiving products on the Internet.

EMBEZZLEMENT Taking of property by someone to whom it has been entrusted.

ENTREPRENEUR A person who is beginning in the business world and understands the responsibility, risks, and rewards of a business.

ESOP Employee Stock Ownership Plan.

EXCLUSIVE TERRITORY A franchiser cannot sell other franchises in an area where the franchisee has the territory right.

EXPENDITURE Amount spent on goods and services.

F

FABRICATED Made up in order to deceive.

FAIR MARKET VALUE What a qualified buyer will pay for goods, services, or property.

FAQ Frequently asked questions.

FEDERAL TAX IDENTIFICATION NUMBER A number assigned to a corporation for tax purposes.

FEDERAL TRADE COMMISSION The branch of the government that regulates franchising.

FINANCIAL STATEMENTS A balance sheet and income statement that may include cash flow reports to indicate a company's financial condition.

FISCAL YEAR A 12-month period that does not correlate with a calendar year.

FIXED BUDGET Budget figures based on a definite level of activity.

FIXED EMPLOYEES
Employees who are necessary no matter the volume of business.

FLIGHT The period of an advertiser's campaign.

FRANCHISE An arrangement for the rights of a particular trademark, trade name, product, and copyright to be used in a certain location for a certain amount of time.

FRANCHISE CONGLOMERATE A franchiser that deals with several different chains.

FRANCHISE CONSULTANT A consultant who assists in choosing which franchise is a good fit with the prospective franchisee.

FRANCHISE FEE A fee paid to the franchiser by the franchisee to begin the franchise.

FRANCHISE LAWYER A lawyer who specializes in franchising.

FRANCHISEE The person who owns one or more franchises and has the right to conduct business as granted by a franchiser.

FRANCHISING A method of doing business that allows a corporation to expand.

FRANCHISER The owner of the franchise who grants franchisees the rights to sell its products and use its name.

G

GENERAL PARTNERSHIP A partnership in which each of the partners is liable for all of the business's debt.

GROSS SALES The amount of sales made before expenses are deducted.

H

HEADQUARTERS The central office for a corporation or franchise.

HOLDING COMPANY A company controlling partial or complete interest in another company or other companies.

HR DEPARTMENT Human resources department; takes care of payroll, training, hiring, and terminating.

I

INCOME STATEMENT A statement showing the profit or loss of a business.

INCORPORATION Creating a new corporation.

INCORPORATOR The person

who takes care of all the legal aspects of incorporation and signs the articles of incorporation.

INDUSTRY The specific branch of manufacture and trade.

INITIAL INVESTMENT The total investment made at the startup of a business required to begin operating a franchise.

INITIAL PUBLIC OFFERING Initial public issuance of stock for a corporation.

INTERNAL CONTROLS Methods and policies designed to prevent fraud, minimize errors, promote operating efficiency, and achieve compliance with established policies.

INTERNATIONAL FRANCHISE ASSOCIATION Trade organization for franchisers.

INVENTORY CONTROL System used for establishing the physical presence of all objects for which a business has custody.

INVOICE Shows prices and amount of goods sent to a purchaser for payment; a bill.

J

JOB ANALYSIS Job description and specifications.

JOB SHARING Two people share the responsibilities and hours of one position.

JOB SPECIFICATIONS The qualifications needed to hold a job; includes educational, physical and mental requirements.

JUST-IN-TIME Having inventory delivered just in time for assembly.

L

LABOR COSTS Total expenses an employer must meet in order to retain the services of employees.

LEAST COMPENSATION SYSTEM A system to receive compensation from a franchiser when economical problems occur.

LIABILITY Debt owed by the company.

LICENSE-REQUIRED FRANCHISE A franchise where the owner must possess a license to start the business.

LIMITED LIABILITY COMPANY A business structure created so that the owners are only liable to the extent of their contribution.

LIMITED PARTNERSHIP A partnership in which some

of the partners have a limited liability to the firm's creditors.

LIQUIDATION The sale of assets to pay off debts.

LOCATION The site where the franchise will operate.

LOGO Trademark.

LOSS CONTROL Attempting to prevent losses.

M

MANUAL Guidebook for employees and managers outlining the company policy.

MARGIN The difference between the cost and the selling price.

MARKETING Means by which an outlet is exposed to the public.

MARKETING PLAN A business plan, marketing strategy, and anticipated expansion of the franchise.

MASTER FRANCHISEE The right for the franchisee to act as a franchiser to create and sell franchises within the franchisee's territory.

MASTER REGION The area within which the master franchisee is in control of and has the rights to re-sell franchises.

MEGA-FRANCHISER A large number of chains owned by one franchiser.

MEMBER A person who is part or complete owner of the company.

MEMBERSHIP GUIDEBOOK A book that describes to the franchisee how the franchise should be run.

MEMBERSHIP INTEREST A member's ownership is represented by "interests."

MERGER When two corporations join to become one.

MINORITY-OWNED BUSINESS Business where the sole proprietor is a minority, or, in the case of multiple owners, where 51 percent of the stock interest claims or rights are held by minorities.

MINUTES A written account of what transpired at a meeting.

MLM (Multi-Level Marketing) A way that a company sells their product by using a network of distributors.

MODEL BUDGET Detailed information about the income and expenses of the business.

MONETARY To do with paper notes or coinage.

MOONLIGHTING The holding

of more than one paid job at the same time by a single individual.

MULTI-UNIT FRANCHISE
An agreement that allows the franchisee the right to create more than one unit.

N

NATIONAL ALLIANCE OF FRANCHISEES A national organization that protects the rights of franchisees.

NATIONAL CHAIN A countrywide company that has branches throughout the nation.

NET CASH FLOW The revenue remaining after costs, interest, and debts are paid.

NET PURCHASE PRICE The price paid by the company for one unit.

NET WORTH The difference between total assets and liabilities.

NON-COMPETE CLAUSE An agreement that prohibits the competition of the same line of business after termination, sale, or transfer.

NON-STORE BUSINESS A business that is established without opening any actual stores.

NO-PAR-VALUE STOCK A stock with no designated face value.

NORENWAKE-SYSTEM
A system in which an employee retires from a firm but maintains a business relationship with the former employer.

NOT-FOR-PROFIT (OR NONPROFIT) CORPORATION
A corporation that does not take a profit; usually organized for charity.

O

OFFER A proposal to sell a franchise to a prospective franchisee.

OFFICERS People who are responsible for the daily operations of a business.

OPERATING BUDGET
Detailed revenue and expense plan for a determined period.

OPERATIONS MANUAL A guidebook that describes how the franchise should be run.

ORGANIZATIONAL MEETING A meeting where the establishment of the corporation is completed.

ORGANIZER Someone who prepares all the documents for the business.

OUTSOURCING A system of using sub-contractors rather than hired employees.

OVERHEAD The monthly expenses that remain the same regardless of sales.

OWNER The person who possesses complete control over the business.

P

PAID-IN CAPITAL The capital received from investors in exchange for stock.

PARENT CORPORATION A corporation that owns controlling interest in another corporation.

PARTNERSHIP A business entity that is composed of two or more people.

PAR-VALUE The amount that an issuer agrees to repay at the date of maturity of a bond; also called face value.

PAYROLL SERVICE PROVIDER A company not affiliated with the corporation that handles the payroll and other payroll-related tasks.

PENALTY FOR CONTRACT BREACH A penalty that must be paid because of breaking a contract.

PERCENTAGE RENT The percentage of the sales volume calculates the rent.

PERSONAL GUARANTY A request from a lender to the owner of a corporation in case the corporation should fail.

PILOT OPERATION A test of a business plan to see if the business would work.

POS Point-of-sale system.

POSTING Placing brochures in customer's mailbox.

POWER OF ATTORNEY The authorization of an attorney to act as a representative.

PRIVILEGED PRODUCT A product that is superior to that of other chains.

PRO FORMA A balance sheet, profit and loss or cash flow statement which estimates income and expense sources.

PROCEDURE The method of doing a task.

PRODUCT FORMAT FRANCHISE When a franchiser allows a distributor to sell their product but does not limit them to just their product.

PROFIT & LOSS STATEMENT A statement showing the income and expenses of the business.

PROHIBITION OF PURSUING A COMPETING BUSINESS The prevention of running two competing franchises at the same time.

PROMPT PAYMENT ACT Requires by law that federal agencies pay interest to companies on unpaid bills over 30-days old.

PROPRIETORSHIP Ownership.

PROTECTED TERRITORY A franchiser agrees with the franchisee to sell no other franchises in the area.

PROXY Written or electronic means used by a shareholder to authorize someone else to vote on their behalf.

PUBLIC FIGURE INVOLVEMENT The disclosure of a well-known public figure endorsing the franchiser's product.

Q

QUALIFICATION QUESTIONNAIRE A document completed by a prospective franchisee which provides the franchiser enough information to decide whether the prospect is capable and motivated.

QUALITY CONTROL The method by which the franchiser enforces the rules set forth in the operating manual and ensures the consistency of the franchise.

QUALITY STANDARDS High standards set during training so that the franchise can enhance its image with each new franchisee.

QUORUM The required number of shareholders or directors to conduct business at a meeting.

R

RANKING METHOD Ranks each job relative to all other jobs.

REAL PROPERTY All immovable property such as land and buildings or other objects permanently affixed to the land.

RECEIPT A written acknowledgement that something has been received.

REGISTRATION Documents that must be filed with the state before a franchise is allowed to be offered in that state.

REINSTATEMENT The return of a corporation that had formerly been dissolved.

RENEWAL A re-signing of the franchise agreement when the past contract expires.

REQUISITION To apply for something needed.

RESOLUTION A decision made

by the shareholders or board of directors.

RESOURCE CENTER An explanation of the franchise being considered.

RETRO FRANCHISING A franchise that is sold by the franchiser because the franchiser no longer wishes to run the specific location.

RISK The possibility that actual outcomes may differ from those expected.

ROYALTY A percentage of the gross sale, final profit or fixed amount that is paid to the franchiser on a regular basis.

RULES OF OPERATION Rules by which a franchisee must run the company.

S

S.C.O.R.E. Service Corps of Retired Executives; a nonprofit organization that provides small business counseling.

SALARY A regular payment for services rendered.

SALES PREDICTION An estimate of the sales based on a new or existing store.

SALES PROMOTION PRODUCT A product that is sold to increase sales and promote the business.

SBA Small Business Administration.

SCALE MERIT Measurement of merit based on the increase of sales of a business.

SECTOR A group of securities that share common characteristics.

SECURED CREDIT A loan for which the borrower pledges collateral.

SHARE The ownership or interest in a corporation.

SHAREHOLDER Someone who owns shares in the corporation.

SHELF COMPANY A company that is formed but has no activity.

SHRINKAGE Shoplifting and other types of theft that create a loss of goods.

SIMPLE INTEREST Interest accumulated on the principal of a loan.

SITE CRITERIA A standard on which a decision for a location can be based.

SLICK A pre-prepared advertisement for the franchisee prepared by the franchiser.

SOLE PROPRIETORSHIP A business that is run by only one individual.

STANDARD INDUSTRIAL CLASSIFICATION A system that classifies businesses to an industry.

STATED CAPITAL Outstanding shares multiplied by the par value of shares.

STOCK Ownership in a corporation.

STOCK CERTIFICATE A document stating proof of ownership of stock in a corporation.

STOCK OPTION The right to purchase a stated number of shares in a company at today's price at a future time.

STOCK TRANSFER BOOK A record that shows the owners of shares of stock in a corporation.

STORE BUSINESS A business that is created with stores that are already in place and ready for use.

SUB-Franchiser When a franchisee acts a franchiser and re-sells the franchise within his territory.

SUBSIDIARY A company whose voting stock is more than 50 percent controlled by another company, usually referred to as the parent company.

SURETY BONDS A guarantee of reimbursement even if a company fails to complete a contract.

SWEAT EQUITY Value added to real estate by owners who make improvements of their own effort.

SWEEP ACCOUNT Funds that are not being used in a low-interest account may be swept to a high-interest account overnight, or longer, to maximize the interest earned.

T

TAX NUMBER The number assigned to businesses by a state revenue department that enables the business to buy wholesale without paying sales tax.

TAX-EXEMPT ORGANIZATION An organization that is not required by law to pay taxes on any income.

TERRITORIAL SERVICE Delivery at consumer's home.

TERRITORY SYSTEM A system where a business is given exclusive rights to sell goods in a specified territory.

TOTAL INVESTMENT The entire amount needed to start a franchise.

TRADE AREA An area from where 60 percent to 80 percent of sales originate.

TRADE SECRET Knowledge that is passed from the franchiser to the franchisee exclusive to the franchise.

TRADEMARK A logo that is protected against other's use.

TREASURY SHARES Stocks that were re-purchased by the company from the shareholder.

TRIPLE NET A type of rental in which the business pays all costs of the building in addition to rent.

TURNKEY A business that is ready for use where the new owner has practically no startup costs.

TYING Forcing a franchisee to purchase one product as a condition to the sale of another.

U

UNIFORM FRANCHISE OFFERING CIRCULAR OR DOCUMENT Contains key information on franchise fees and startup costs.

UNDERWRITER An investment bank that guarantees prices on securities to corporations.

UNSECURED CREDIT A no-collateral loan.

V

VARIABLE COST The cost of doing business that is directly related to the sales of goods or services.

VENTURE CAPITAL Money used to support new or unusual commercial ventures.

VENTURE COMPANY A new business that involves high risk and uncertainty.

VOLUNTARY DISSOLUTION The decision to dissolve a corporation, made by the shareholders or directors.

VOTING RIGHTS The right of shareholders to use their ownership of stock to vote.

W

WASTE LOSS Products that were disposed of because they could not be sold.

WOMEN-OWNED BUSINESS A business that is controlled 51 percent by women and includes government advantages and low-interest loans.

WORKING CAPITAL The difference between current assets and current liabilities; used to evaluate the liquidity of a company.

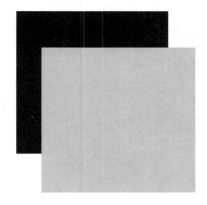

Index